CIMA Exam Practice Kit

C000060607

Management Accounting Performance Evaluation

CIMA Exam Practice Kit

Management Accounting Performance Evaluation

Bob Scarlett

ELSEVIER   Amsterdam • Boston • Heidelberg • London • New York •
Oxford Paris • San Diego • San Francisco • Singapore • Sydney •

CIMA Publishing
An imprint of Elsevier
Linacre House, Jordan Hill, Oxford OX2 8DP
30 Corporate Drive, Burlington, MA 01803

First published 2008

British Library Cataloguing in Publication Data
A catalogue record for this book is available from the British Library

978 0 7506 8669 3

For information on all CIMA Publishing Publications
visit our website at www.cimapublishing.com

Typeset by Integra Software Services Pvt. Ltd, Pondicherry, India
www.integra-india.com
Printed and bound in Hungary

Working together to grow
libraries in developing countries

www.elsevier.com | www.bookaid.org | www.sabre.org

ELSEVIER   BOOK AID
International   Sabre Foundation

Contents

Syllabus Guidance, Learning Objectives and Verbs

A The syllabus

The syllabus for the CIMA Professional Chartered Management Accounting qualification 2005 comprises three learning pillars:

- Management Accounting pillar
- Business Management pillar
- Financial Management pillar.

Within each learning pillar there are three syllabus subjects. Two of these subjects are set at the lower "Managerial" level, with the third subject positioned at the higher "Strategic" level. All subject examinations have a duration of three hours and the pass mark is 50%.

Note: In addition to these nine examinations, students are required to gain three years relevant practical experience and successfully sit the Test of Professional Competence in Management Accounting (TOPCIMA).

B Aims of the syllabus

The aims of the syllabus are:

- To provide for the Institute, together with the practical experience requirements, an adequate basis for assuring society that those admitted to membership are competent to act as management accountants for entities, whether in manufacturing, commercial or service organisations, in the public or private sectors of the economy.
- To enable the Institute to examine whether prospective members have an adequate knowledge, understanding and mastery of the stated body of knowledge and skills.
- To complement the Institute's practical experience and skills development requirements.

C Study weightings

A percentage weighting is shown against each topic in the syllabus. This is intended as a guide to the proportion of study time each topic requires.

All topics in the syllabus must be studied, since any single examination question may examine more than one topic, or carry a higher proportion of marks than the percentage study time suggested.

The weightings *do not* specify the number of marks that will be allocated to topics in the examination.

D Learning outcomes

Each topic within the syllabus contains a list of learning outcomes, which should be read in conjunction with the knowledge content for the syllabus. A learning outcome has two main purposes:

1   to define the skill or ability that a well-prepared candidate should be able to exhibit in the examination;
2   to demonstrate the approach likely to be taken by examiners in examination questions.

The learning outcomes are part of a hierarchy of learning objectives. The verbs used at the beginning of each learning outcome relate to a specific learning objective, for example, evaluate alternative approaches to budgeting.

The verb "evaluate" indicates a high-level learning objective. As learning objectives are hierarchical, it is expected that at this level, students will have knowledge of different budgeting systems and methodologies and be able to apply them.

A list of the learning objectives and the verbs that appear in the syllabus learning outcomes and examinations, follows:

Learning objective	*Verbs used*	*Definition*
1 Knowledge		
What you are expected to know	List	Make a list of
	State	Express, fully or clearly, the details of/ facts of
	Define	Give the exact meaning of
2 Comprehension		
What you are expected to understand	Describe	Communicate the key features of
	Distinguish	Highlight the differences between
	Explain	Make clear or intelligible/State the meaning of
	Identify	Recognise, establish or select after consideration
	Illustrate	Use an example to describe or explain something

3 Application

How you are expected to apply your knowledge

Apply	To put to practical use
Calculate/ compute	To ascertain or reckon mathematically
Demonstrate	To prove with certainty or to exhibit by practical means
Prepare	To make or get ready for use
Reconcile	To make or prove consistent/ compatible
Solve	Find an answer to
Tabulate	Arrange in a table

4 Analysis

How you are expected to analyse the detail of what you have learned

Analyse	Examine in detail the structure of
Categorise	Place into a defined class or division
Compare and contrast	Show the similarities and/or differences between
Construct	To build up or compile
Discuss	To examine in detail by argument
Interpret	To translate into intelligible or familiar terms
Produce	To create or bring into existence

5 Evaluation

How you are expected to use your learning to evaluate, make decisions or recommendations

Advise	To counsel, inform or notify
Evaluate	To appraise or assess the value of
Recommend	To advise on a course of action

Learning Outcomes, Syllabus Content and Examination Format

Paper P1 – Management Accounting Performance Evaluation

Syllabus outline

The syllabus comprises:

Topic and study weighting

- A Cost Accounting Systems   25%
- B Standard Costing   25%
- C Budgeting   30%
- D Control and Performance
    Measurement of Responsibility Centres 20%

Learning aims

Students should be able to:

- apply both traditional and contemporary approaches to cost accounting in a variety of contexts and evaluate the impact of "modern" data processing and processing technologies such as MRP, ERP and JIT;
- explain and apply the principles of standard costing, calculate variances in a variety of contexts and critically evaluate the worth of standard costing in the light of contemporary criticisms;
- develop budgets using both traditional and contemporary techniques, evaluate both interactive and diagnostic uses of budgets in a variety of contexts and discuss the issues raised by those that advocate techniques "beyond budgeting";
- prepare appropriate financial statements for cost, profit and investment centre managers, calculate appropriate financial performance indicators, assess the impact of alternative transfer pricing policies and discuss the behavioural consequences of management control systems based on responsibility accounting, decentralisation and delegation.

Assessment strategy

There will be a written examination paper of three hours, with the following sections.

Section A – 40 marks
> A variety of compulsory objective test questions, each worth between 2 and 4 marks. Mini-scenarios may be given, to which a group of questions relate.

Section B – 30 marks
> Six compulsory short answer questions, each worth 5 marks. A short scenario may be given, to which some or all questions relate.

Section C – 30 marks
> One question, from a choice of two, worth 20 marks. Short scenarios may be given, to which questions relate.

A – Cost accounting systems – 25%

Learning outcomes

On completion of their studies students should be able to:

1 compare and contrast marginal and absorption costing methods in respect of profit reporting and stock valuation;

2 apply marginal and absorption costing approaches in job, batch and process environments;

3 prepare ledger accounts according to context: marginal or absorption based in job, batch or process environments, including work-in-progress and related accounts such as production overhead control account and abnormal loss account;

4 explain the origins of throughput accounting as "super variable costing" and its application as a variant of marginal or variable cost accounting;

5 apply standard costing methods within costing systems and demonstrate the reconciliation of budgeted and actual profit margins;

6 compare activity-based costing with traditional marginal and absorption costing methods and evaluate its potential as a system of cost accounting;

7 explain the role of MRP and ERP systems in supporting standard costing systems, calculating variances and facilitating the posting of ledger entries;

8 evaluate the impact of just-in-time manufacturing methods on cost accounting and the use of "back-flush accounting" when work-in-progress stock is minimal.

Syllabus content

- Marginal (or variable) costing as a system of profit reporting and stock valuation.
- Absorption costing as a system of profit reporting and stock valuation.
- Throughput accounting as a system of profit reporting and stock valuation.
- Activity-based costing as a potential system of profit reporting and stock valuation.
- The integration of standard costing with marginal cost accounting, absorption cost accounting and throughput accounting.
- Process accounting including establishment of equivalent units in stock, work-in-progress and abnormal loss accounts and the use of first-in first-out, average cost and standard cost methods of stock valuation.
- MRP and ERP systems for resource planning and the integration of accounting functions with other systems, such as purchase ordering and production planning.
- Back-flush accounting in just-in-time production environments. The benefits of just-in-time production, total quality management and theory of constraints and the possible impacts of these methods on cost accounting and performance measurement.

B – Standard costing – 25%

Learning outcomes

On completion of their studies students should be able to:

1 explain why and how standards are set in manufacturing and in service industries with particular reference to the maximisation of efficiency and minimisation of waste;
2 calculate and interpret material, labour, variable overhead, fixed overhead and sales variances;
3 prepare and discuss a report which reconciles budget and actual profit using absorption and/or marginal costing principles;
4 calculate and explain planning and operational variances;
5 prepare reports using a range of internal and external benchmarks and interpret the results;
6 discuss the behavioural implications of setting standard costs.

Syllabus content

- Manufacturing standards for material, labour, variable overhead and fixed overhead.
- Price/rate and usage/efficiency variances for materials, labour and variable overhead. Further subdivision of total usage/efficiency variances into mix and yield components. (*Note*: The calculation of mix variances on both individual and average valuation bases is required.)
- Fixed overhead expenditure and volume variances. (*Note*: The subdivision of fixed overhead volume variance into capacity and efficiency elements will not be examined.)
- Planning and operational variances.
- Standards and variances in servicing industries (including the phenomenon of "McDonaldization"), public services (e.g. Health) (including the use of "diagnostic related" or "reference" groups), and the professions (e.g. labour mix variances in audit work). Criticisms of standard costing in general and in advanced manufacturing environments in particular.
- Sales price and sales revenue/margin volume variances (calculation of the latter on a unit basis related to revenue, gross margin and contribution margin). Application of these variances to all sectors, including professional services and retail analysis.
- Interpretation of variances: interrelationship, significance.
- Benchmarking.
- Behavioural implications of setting standard costs.

C – Budgeting – 30%

Learning outcomes

On completion of their studies students should be able to:

1 explain why organisations prepare forecasts and plans;
2 calculate projected product/service volumes employing appropriate forecasting techniques;
3 calculate projected revenues and costs based on product/service volumes, pricing strategies and cost structures;
4 evaluate projected performance by calculating key metrics including profitability, liquidity and asset turnover ratios;
5 describe and explain the possible purposes of budgets, including planning, communication, co-ordination, motivation, authorisation, control and evaluation;

6 evaluate and apply alternative approaches to budgeting;

7 calculate the consequences of "what-if" scenarios and evaluate their impact on master profit and loss account and balance sheet;

8 explain the concept of responsibility accounting and its importance in the construction of functional budgets that support the overall master budget;

9 identify controllable and uncontrollable costs in the context of responsibility accounting and explain why "uncontrollable" costs may or may not be allocated to responsibility centres;

10 explain the ideas of feedback and feed-forward control and their application in the use of budgets for control;

11 evaluate performance using fixed and flexible budget reports;

12 discuss the role of non-financial performance indicators and compare and contrast traditional approaches to budgeting with recommendations based on the "balanced scorecard";

13 evaluate the impact of budgetary control systems on human behaviour;

14 evaluate the criticisms of budgeting particularly from the advocates of techniques that are "beyond budgeting".

Syllabus content

- Time series analysis including moving totals and averages, treatment of seasonality, trend analysis using regression analysis and the application of these techniques in forecasting product and service volumes.
- Fixed, variable, semi-variable and activity-based categorisations of cost and their application in projecting financial results.
- What-if analysis based on alternate projections of volumes, prices and cost structures and the use of spreadsheets in facilitating these analyses.
- The purposes of budgets and conflicts that can arise (e.g. between budgets for realistic planning and budgets based on "hard to achieve" targets for motivation).
- The creation of budgets including incremental approaches, zero-based budgeting and activity-based budgets.
- The use of budgets in planning: "rolling budgets" for adaptive planning.
- The use of budgets for control: controllable costs and variances based on "fixed" and "flexed" budgets. The conceptual link between standard costing and budget flexing.
- Behavioural issues in budgeting: participation in budgeting and its possible beneficial consequences for ownership and motivation; participation in budgeting and its possible adverse consequences for "budget padding" and manipulation; setting budget targets for motivation etc.
- Criticisms of budgeting and the recommendations of the advocates of the balanced scorecard and "beyond budgeting".

D – Control and performance measurement of responsibility centres – 20%

Learning outcomes

On completion of their studies students should be able to:

1 discuss the use of cost, revenue, profit and investment centres in devising organisation structure and in management control;

2 prepare cost information in appropriate formats for cost centre managers, taking due account of controllable/uncontrollable costs and the importance of budget flexing;

3   prepare revenue and cost information in appropriate formats for profit and investment centre managers, taking due account of cost variability, attributable costs, controllable costs and identification of appropriate measures of profit centre "contribution";

4   calculate and apply measures of performance for investment centres (often "strategic business units" or divisions of larger groups);

5   discuss the likely behavioural consequences of the use of performance metrics in managing cost, profit and investment centres;

6   explain the typical consequences of a divisional structure for performance measurement as divisions compete or trade with each other;

7   identify the likely consequences of different approaches to transfer pricing for divisional decision-making, divisional and group profitability, the motivation of divisional management and the autonomy of individual divisions.

Syllabus content

- Organisation structure and its implications for responsibility accounting.

- Presentation of financial information including issues of controllable/uncontrollable costs, variable/fixed costs and tracing revenues and costs to particular cost objects.

- Return on investment and its deficiencies; the emergence of residual income and economic value added to address these.

- Behavioural issues in the application of performance measures in cost, profit and investment centres.

- The theory of transfer pricing, including perfect, imperfect and no market for the intermediate good.

- Use of negotiated, market, cost-plus and variable cost-based transfer prices. "Dual" transfer prices and lump sum payments as means of addressing some of the issues that arise.

- The interaction of transfer pricing and tax liabilities in international operations and implications for currency management and possible distortion of internal company operations in order to comply with Tax Authority directives.

Examination Techniques

Essay questions

Your essay should have a clear structure, that is, an introduction, a middle and an end. Think in terms of 1 mark for each relevant point made.

Numerical questions

It is essential to show workings in your answer. If you come up with the wrong answer and no workings, the examiner cannot award any marks. However, if you get the wrong answer but apply the correct technique then you will be given some marks.

Reports and memorandum

Where you are asked to produce an answer in a report type format you will be given easy marks for style and presentation.

- A *report* is a document from an individual or group in one organisation sent to an individual or group in another.
- A *memorandum* is an informal report going from one individual or group to another individual or group in the same organisation.

You should start a report as follows:

To: J. SMITH, CEO, ABC plc

From: M ACCOUNTANT

Date: 31 December 2000

Terms of Reference: Financial Strategy of ABC plc

Multiple choice questions managerial level

From May 2005 some multiple choice questions will be worth more than two marks. Even if you get answer wrong, you may still get some marks for technique. Therefore show all workings on such questions.

Marginal and Absorption Costing

Marginal and Absorption Costing

1

The cost per unit of an item is important for

- setting the selling price
- valuing stocks
- calculating profitability.

Marginal costing

The cost of an item includes only the variable costs incurred in its production. For example, Material components used and piece-rate assembly labour costs.

Accounting entries

As costs are incurred (e.g. materials)

Dr Material Stock Account
Cr Creditors (or cash) Account

As materials are issued to production

Dr Process 1 Account
Cr Material Stock Account

Direct labour costs are treated similarly.

Fixed production overheads are taken straight to the P&L at the year end.

Absorption costing

The cost of an item includes the variable costs incurred in its production *and* a proportion of production overheads.

Thus,
absorption cost (AC) = marginal cost (MC) + some fixed overhead (FO)

The fixed overhead per unit is the absorption rate (FOAR).

Possible bases (methods) for sharing out the fixed overheads include

- units
- labour hours
- machine hours
- material usage.

Accounting entries

All variable production costs are recorded as for marginal costing.

In addition, the fixed overhead per unit is transferred to the process account.

This gives rise to an under or over absorption of fixed overheads; that is, a balance on the fixed overhead account which is taken to the profit and loss account.

Reconciliation: marginal costing and absorption costing

Marginal costing profit and absorption costing profit are the same apart from the impact of fixed overheads on stock.

They can be reconciled thus

Profit per AC	£x
Add: FO in opening stock	£x
Less: FO in closing stock	£(x)
Profit per MC	£xx

Comparison: MC vs AC

MC	AC
Good for short-term decision-making	Consistent with external accounting
Profit not distorted by stock policy	Prices must cover all costs
Treats fixed costs as period costs	Highlights total cost of producing

? Questions

1.1 A company has budgeted production of 500 X's and 300 Y's next year. Y's take twice as long to make as X's.

Total fixed overheads are expected to be £102,000.

Costs relating to the X are budgeted at

Materials:	3,000 kg	£24,000
Labour:	2,000 hours	£40,000

Fixed overheads are to be absorbed on an hourly basis.

In addition to the above some material normally goes to waste, this is expected to amount to 10% of materials purchased.

What is the absorption cost per unit of X?

A   £225.52
B   £226.05
C   £260.30
D   £260.83

(4 marks)

1.2   A company's production and sales were budgeted at 300 units.

Actual production was 315 but sales were only 295.

The marginal cost profit was

	£	£
Sales		64,900
COS		
Materials	15,750	
Labour	15,750	
	31,500	
Closing stock	2,000	
		29,500
		35,400
Fixed overheads		9,000
Net profit		26,400

All costs were in line with expectations.
There was no opening stock.

What would the under/over absorption of overheads have been if the company had used absorption costing?

A   £150   Under absorbed
B   £150   Over absorbed
C   £450   Under absorbed
D   £450   Over absorbed

(2 marks)

1.3   A company is considering improving its quality system leading to an improved reputation and eventually a higher selling price.

Its current costs are shown below:

	Old system	New system
Total demand	3,600 units	3,600 units
Defective production	20%	10%
Labour cost per unit produced	£35	£43
Total material per unit	3.2 kg	3.5 kg
Price per kg of material	£3.20	£3.95
Overheads	£18,000	£29,560

Which of the following is closest to the increase in selling price needed to justify this change?

A £3.20
B £9.80
C £11.40
D £15.00

(4 marks)

1.4 A company budgeted to produce and sell equal numbers of units. In fact production was above budget whilst sales were below budget.

Which of the following statements about marginal costing and absorption costing profits is most likely to be true?

A absorption costing profits will be higher than marginal costing profits
B absorption costing profits will be equal to marginal costing profits
C absorption costing profits will be lower than marginal costing profits
D absorption costing profits could be higher or lower or equal to marginal costing profits

(2 marks)

1.5 The following are claimed to be advantages of marginal costing over absorption costing.

(i) Marginal costing avoids arbitrary sharing of costs.
(ii) Marginal costing is better for short-term decision-making.
(iii) Marginal costing avoids profit distortions due to stock fluctuations.

Which of these claims are substantially true?

A (i) and (ii) only
B (ii) and (iii) only
C (i) and (iii) only
D all of them

(2 marks)

1.6 The following details have been extracted from the budget papers of LK plc for June 2003:

Selling price per unit	£124
Variable production costs per unit	£54
Fixed production costs per unit	£36
Other variable costs per unit	£12
Sales volume	12,500 units
Production volume	13,250 units
Opening stock of finished items	980 units

If budgeted profit statements were prepared by using absorption costing and then by using marginal costing,

A marginal costing profits would be higher by £27,000.
B absorption costing profits would be higher by £27,000.
C absorption costing profits would be higher by £35,000.
D absorption costing profits would be higher by £62,000.

(2 marks)

1.7 The following are the results of last year's production.

Budgeted overheads = £8,000
Budgeted production = 4,000 units
Actual overheads = £8,500
Actual production = 3,800 units

What is the over/under absorption?

A £500 under absorption
B £500 over absorption
C £900 under absorption
D £900 over absorption

(2 marks)

1.8 A company's cost card is shown below.

	£
Materials	10
Labour	15
Fixed overheads	8
	33
Variable selling costs	7
	40
Selling price	50
Profit	10

Last year 4,000 units were produced, of which 3,750 were sold. Actual fixed overheads were £28,000. There was no opening stock.

Calculate the profits under marginal costing and absorption costing, and reconcile them.

(5 marks)

1.9 In what situations is absorption costing more appropriate than marginal costing?

Are there any situations where marginal costing is more appropriate?

(5 marks)

✅ Answers

1.1 **B**

Note that material cost given represents only 90% of total costs and must be increased by a factor of 10/9.

The overheads must be shared between the products using labour hours (2,000 ÷ 500 = 4 hours for an X and therefore 8 hours for a Y).

	£
Material cost: £24,000 × 10/9 = £26,667	
Per unit (£26,667 ÷ 500)	53.33
Labour cost per unit (£40,000 ÷ 500)	80.00
FO per unit	
Total hours: X + Y	
500 × 4 hours + 300 × 8 hours = 4,400 hours	
Overheads per hour: £102,000 ÷ 4,400 = £23.18	
Per unit of X (£23.18 × 4 hours)	92.72
AC per unit	226.05 = B

If you simply added 10% to the material cost then it comes to £52.80 (reducing overall cost to £225.52 = A).

If you used units to absorb the overheads this gives £127.50 per unit (increasing overall cost to £260.83 = D).

Both of these errors give £260.30 = C.

1.2 **D**

Overheads would be over absorbed since actual production was higher than budget.

Remember to use production as a basis for absorption, not sales.

Budgeted FO per unit = £9,000 ÷ 300 units = £30.00

	£
Absorbed (£30.00 × 315)	9,450
Spent	9,000
Over absorbed	450 = D

If you use sales to absorb then you would calculate an under absorption of £30.00 × 295 − £9,000 = £150 = A.

1.3 **B**

In the following only the workings for the old system are shown. The new system would be similar.

Remember that if sales are to be 3,600 units and 20% of production is defective then only 80% of production is available to be sold. Total production needs to be 100/80 × 3,600 = 4,500 units.

If you calculate defects as 20% × 3,600 = 720 and total production as 3,600 + 720 = 4,320, then when you lose 20% × 4,320 = 864 there are only 4,320 − 864 = 3,456 available for sale.

	Old system	New system
Total demand	3,600 units	3,600 units
Defective production	20%	10%
Total production required (3,600 × 100/80)	4,500 units	4,000 units
Labour cost (£35 × 4,500)	£157,500	£172,000
Material cost (4,500 × 3.2 kg × £3.20)	£46,080	£55,300
Overheads	£18,000	£29,560
Total costs (157,500 + 46,080 + 18,000)	£221,580	£256,860
Cost per unit (221,580 ÷ 3,600)	£61.55	£71.35

Increase in cost per unit = £71.35 − £61.55 = £9.80.

1.4 A

In this case stocks will rise and thus absorption costing will carry forward some overheads to the next period.

Thus absorption costing profits will be higher.

1.5 D

All of these are true.

(i) Absorption costing has to share fixed costs in an arbitrary manner.
(ii) Selling prices need to exceed only variable costs in the short term.
(iii) Absorption costing causes profit distortions with stock fluctuations.

1.6 B

Remember that profits will be higher under AC since production > sales and so some of this year's overheads will be carried forward in stock and charged against next year's income.

It is only production overheads that this applies to.

Increase in stocks = 13,250 − 12,500 = 750 units
Extra overheads c/f = 750 × £36 = £27,000 = B.

1.7 C

Always work out the absorption rate before you start an absorption costing question.

Absorption rate = £8,000/4,000 = £2 per unit

Total overhead absorbed = £2 × 3,800 units = £7,600

Total amount spent = £8,500

Under absorption = £8,500 − £7,600 = £900.

1.8

Remember to value stocks correctly: include the fixed overheads only in absorption costing.

Marginal cost = £25, absorption cost = £33

	Unit	MC		AC	
	£	£	£	£	£
Sales	50		187,500		187,500
COS					
Materials	10	40,000		40,000	
Labour	15	60,000		60,000	
FO	0/8	–		32,000	
		100,000		132,000	
Closing stock	25/33	(6,250)		(8,250)	
			93,750		123,750
			93,750		63,750
FO			(28,000)		
Over absorption					4,000
			65,750		67,750
Selling costs	7		(26,250)		(26,250)
Profit			39,500		41,500

Reconciliation

	£
Profit per AC	41,500
Less: FO in closing stock (£8 × 250 units)	(2,000)
Profit per MC	39,500

1.9 Absorption costing is more appropriate in the following situations.

- *Long-run pricing.* In the long run both marginal costs and overheads need to be covered, using absorption costing ensures this will be so.

- *Financial accounting.* The standardisation of external reporting requirements requires that a reasonable proportion of overheads be included in stock valuations. Many companies want the external and internal accounts to reveal the same level of profits.

Where there is only one product the overheads are clearly attributable to that product and the overhead per unit figure is fairly non-controversial.

Marginal costing may be more appropriate where stock building is to be discouraged. This is because absorption costing tends to boost reported profits when stocks rise, encouraging managers to stock build.

Marginal costing is also more appropriate for short-run pricing decisions since any selling price that covers the marginal costing leads to an increase in contribution and hence profit.

Job, Batch and
Process Costing

Job, Batch and Process Costing

2

Job and batch costing

Direct costs are accumulated on cost cards.

Overheads are added according to whether absorption costing or marginal costing is being used.

Process costing

Used for continuous production of identical items.

$$CostPerUnit = \frac{TotalProductionCosts}{TotalUnitsProduced}$$

Losses

Split into normal (expected) losses and abnormal (above those expected) losses.

Normal losses (N/L) are treated as a regular business expense and hence omitted from the number of units produced. Any expected sale proceeds are deducted from costs.

Abnormal losses (A/L) are valued separately as an indicator of performance.

Thus,

$$CostPerUnit = \frac{TotalCosts - SaleOfNormalLosses}{NormalOutput}$$

A negative abnormal loss is called an abnormal gain and is treated opposite to a loss.

Stocks of work in progress

When units are partially complete they are included in the number of units according to their degree of completion, thus 500 units 80% complete would be counted as 400 units. These are often referred to as equivalent units.

The degree of completion may be different as regards each element of costs, these must then be treated separately.

A First In First Out (FIFO) flow of units is normally assumed, thus all costs brought forward in opening stock are allocated to finished goods.

If a weighted average approach is used then costs brought forward in opening stocks are added to general period costs.

✎ Question approach

Full calculation questions are best handled in five steps.

1 Check that all units are accounted for (many people use the units column of the T account for this).
2 Calculate equivalent units (omit N/L). Do this for each cost heading.
3 Calculate cost per unit (using the formula above).
4 Value the process outputs, as required.
5 Complete the question requirements (e.g. T accounts).

? Questions

2.1 A company produces product X in a continuous process.

Normally about 20% of materials are lost in the process and are sold as a solvent for £2 per litre.

In January inputs were 8,500 litres whilst outputs were 7,200 litres. Materials cost £20,000 whilst conversion costs were £45,000.

There were no opening or closing stocks of any kind.

What will the charge for abnormal gains or losses in the profit and loss account?

A £2,824 abnormal gain
B £3,624 abnormal gain
C £3,624 abnormal loss
D £4,424 abnormal gain

(3 marks)

2.2 Job MH32 has used £37,500 of direct costs. In addition it has passed through two departments with the following overheads.

	Assembly	Painting
Annual budget		
Overheads	£184,500	£229,500
Labour hours	20,500	4,500
Machine hours	4,125	8,500
Job MN32		
Labour hours	1,200	280
Machine hours	330	720

Absorption bases are chosen to reflect the degree and nature of activity in a department.

Which of the following is the most likely total cost on the job card for job MH32?

A   £30,240
B   £62,580
C   £67,740
D   £93,900

(2 marks)

2.3   A company produces product Y in a continuous process.

Normally about 15% of materials are lost in the process and are sold as a scrap for £2 per kg.

In January inputs were 4,500 kg whilst outputs were 3,795 kg.
Materials cost £22,000 whilst conversion costs were £44,375.

There were no opening stocks of any kind, but there were closing stocks of 10 kg of scrap; these are expected to be sold as normal. There was no closing stock of Y.

What will be the charge for abnormal gains and losses in the profit and loss account?

A   £450
B   £470
C   £510
D   £570

(3 marks)

2.4   A company makes three products (A, B and C) from a shared process. At present the company uses weights to share the process costs between the products, but there is a possibility of switching to net realisable value.

	A	B	C
Weight	5,000 kg	6,000 kg	9,000 kg
Selling price per kg	£15	£12	£10
Variable post-split costs	£3	£4	£2

There are no stocks.

The following statements have been made concerning the effects of a change from weight to net realisable value as a method joint cost apportionment.

  (i)   The profits of A will fall.
 (ii)   The profits of B will rise.
(iii)   The profits of the company will be unchanged.

Which of the above statements are substantially true?

A   (i) and (ii) only
B   (ii) and (iii) only
C   (i) and (iii) only
D   all of them

(3 marks)

2.5 A company produces widgets in a continuous process.

Normally 25% of units started are damaged in the process and are sold as a scrap for £5 per unit.

In January inputs of 12,000 units were started whilst outputs were 9,700 units. Materials cost £108,300 whilst labour and overheads were £50,700.

There were no opening stocks of any kind. Closing stock consisted of 250 completed widgets only.

What is the nearest value of closing stock?

A £3,800
B £4,000
C £4,100
D £4,400

(3 marks)

2.6 A company operates a process costing system.

In a month it starts 500 units and completes 420.
Costs are £9,400.

Losses are usually 10% of production and are sold for £8 per unit.
There is no stock.

What is the cost per unit?
What is the loss on sale of the abnormal loss?

(5 marks)

2.7 In a job costing environment what are the double entries (nominal ledger entries) for the following? Assume that there are no losses expected.

(i) The issuing of materials to a job.
(ii) Stock still on site at a job at the year end.
(iii) Faulty stock written off after it has been issued to a job.
(iv) Sale proceeds of faulty stock written off after it has been issued to a job.
(v) Underabsorption of overheads at the year end.

(5 marks)

2.8 Process 8 in a multi-process plant has the following results in March:

Opening stock: 300 units, 80% complete as regards materials but 60% complete as regards conversion costs
Value: £8,000
Units transferred from Process 7: 45,000 at £19 each
Material added costs: £346,212
Conversion costs: £299,082
Units completed: 41,700
Closing stock: 480 units, 80% complete as regards material but 70% complete as regards conversion costs
Losses normally at 5% of units transferred from the previous process. These are sold at £2 each (this relates to material added), none of the lost items have been sold at the month end.

All losses (normal and abnormal) will be sold at £2 eventually.
Losses occur at the end of the process.
Stocks move FIFO.

Requirements

Show the Process 8 account for March.
Show the losses accounts for March.

(20 marks)

2.9 PQR plc is a chemical processing company. The company produces a range of solvents by passing materials through a series of processes. The company uses the FIFO valuation method.

In Process 2, the output from Process 1 (XP1) is blended with two other materials (P2A and P2B) to form XP2. It is expected that 10% of any new input to Process 2 (i.e. transfers from Process 1 plus Process 2 materials added) will be immediately lost and that this loss will have no resale value. It is also expected that in addition to the loss, 5% of any new input will form a by-product, Z, which can be sold without additional processing for $2.00 per litre.

Data from Process 2 for April 2003 was as follows:

Opening work in process
Process 2 had 1,200 litres of opening work in process. The value and degree of completion of this was as follows:

	$	% degree of completion
XP1	1,560	100
P2A	1,540	100
P2B	750	100
Conversion costs	3,790	40
	7,640	

Input
During April, the inputs to Process 2 were

	Litre	$
XP1	5,000	15,679
P2A	1,200	6,000
P2B	3,000	4,500
Conversion costs		22,800

Closing work in process
At the end of April, the work in process was 1,450 litres. This was fully complete in respect of all materials but only 30% complete for conversion costs.

Output
The output from Process 2 during April was

	Litre
Z	460
XP2	7,850

Requirements

(a) Prepare the Process 2 account for April 2003.

(16 marks)

(b) Briefly discuss the methods that could be used to split the costs of the process if there were several products appearing as outputs.

(4 marks)

(Total = 20 marks)

✓ Answers

2.1 A

You must know the formula for calculating the cost per unit. Notice that although there are abnormal gains, here you can just treat them as negative abnormal losses.

It is clear that there has been a loss of 1,300 litres in the process. This compares with a normal loss of $20\% \times 8,500 = 1,700$ litres.

We thus say there is a normal loss of 1,700 litres and an abnormal gain of 400 litres.

The calculation of cost per unit is

(costs − sale from normal losses) ÷ (normal output)

$(20,000 + 45,000 - 1,700 \times 2) \div (8,500 - 1,700) = £9.06/\text{litre}$

The abnormal gains have a cost of $400 \times £9.06 = £3,624$

This is offset by the sale proceeds $= £3,624 - 400 \times £2 = £2,824$.

2.2 C

You need to work out absorption rates before proceeding. Assembly seems labour intensive, whilst painting is machine intensive.

	Assembly	*Painting*
Annual budget		
Overheads	£184,500	£229,500
Hours: labour/machine	20,500	8,500
Rate	£9/hour	£27/hour
Job MN32		
Hours: labour/machine	1,200	720
Absorbed	£10,800	£19,440

Total cost $= £10,800 + £19,440 + £37,500 = £67,740$.

2.3 A

You must know the formula for calculating the cost per unit.

It is clear that there has been a loss of 705 kg in the process. This compares with a normal loss of $15\% \times 4,500\ \text{kg} = 675\ \text{kg}$.

We thus say there is a normal loss of 675 kg and an abnormal loss of 30 kg.

The calculation of cost per unit is

(costs − sale from normal losses) ÷ (normal output)

(22,000 + 44,375 − 675 × 2) ÷ (4,500 − 675) = £17/kg

The abnormal losses have a cost of 30 × £17 = £510

This is offset by the sale proceeds = £510 − 30 × £2 = £450

The fact that there are stocks is irrelevant – these will still have to be written down to net realisable value.

2.4 **D**

We are only changing the method of sharing the costs and not the amount shared, so there will be no impact on the company.

	A	B	C	Total
Weight	5,000 kg	6,000 kg	9,000 kg	20,000 kg
Ratio	25%	30%	45%	
Net realisable value/kg	£12	£8	£8	
Total	£60,000	£48,000	£72,000	£180,000
Ratio	33%	27%	40%	
Cost change	Increase	Decrease		
Profit change	Decrease	Increase		

2.5 **B**

You must know the formula for calculating the cost per unit. Note that we do not need abnormal loss information to calculate this.

The normal loss is 25% × 12,000 = 3,000 units.

The calculation of cost per unit is

(costs − sale from normal losses) ÷ (normal output)

(108,300 + 50,700 − 3,000 × 5) ÷ (12,000 − 3,000) = £16/kg

The value of stocks is therefore 250 × £16 = £4,000.

2.6 Make sure you know the formula for cost per unit in a process costing environment.

Total Losses = 500 − 420 = 80 units

N/L = 10% × 500 = 50 units
A/L = 80 − 50 = 30 units

$$Cost\ Per\ Unit = \frac{Total\ Costs - Sale\ Of\ Normal\ Losses}{Normal\ Output}$$

$$CostPerUnit = \frac{9,400 - 50 \times 8}{500 - 50}$$

Cost per unit = £20

A/L costs = £20 × 30 units = £600
A/L sales = £8 × 30 units = £240

A/L loss = £240 − £600 = £360.

2.7 (i) Dr wip a/c (or job a/c etc.)
Cr material (stock) a/c
    – with the value of materials issued

(ii) c/f stock on Cr side of the wip account at year end
b/f stock on Dr side of the wip account in new year
    – with the closing stock value

(iii) Dr losses a/c
Cr wip a/c
    – with the cost of the stock written off

(iv) Dr cash a/c
Cr losses a/c
    – with the amount received

(v) Dr profit and loss a/c
Cr overheads a/c
    – with the underabsorption

Note that the names of some of these accounts may vary.

2.8 1 Total units

Opening stocks	300
Units transferred in	45,000
	45,300
Closing stock	(480)
N/L (5%)	(2,250)
Good output	(41,700)
A/L	870

2 Equivalent units

Units	Total	Previous process	Materials added	Conversion
Opening stocks – to finish	300	–	60	120
Started + finished	41,400	41,400	41,400	41,400
N/L	2,250	–	–	–
A/L	870	870	870	870
Closing stock started	480	480	384	336
Totals	45,300	42,750	42,714	42,726

3 Cost per unit

	£	£	£
Costs for month	855,000	346,212	299,082
Sale of N/L		4,500	
Totals	855,000	341,712	299,082
Cost per unit	20	8	7
Total £35			

4 Valuations

	Units	Cost (£)	Total (£)
Good output			
Opening stock b/f	300		8,000
Opening stock − finish	60	8	480
	120	7	840
Started + finished	41,400	35	1,449,000
			1,458,320
A/L	870	35	30,450
Closing stock	480	20	9,600
	384	8	3,072
	336	7	2,352
			15,024

5 T accounts

Process 8 account

	Units	£		Units	£
Opening stock b/f	300	8,000			
From Process 7	45,000	855,000	Good output	41,700	1,458,320
Material added		346,212	N/L (sale value)	2,250	4,500
Conversion costs		299,082	A/L (cost)	870	30,450
			Closing stock c/f	480	15,024
	45,300	1,508,294		45,300	1,508,294

Abnormal gains and losses account

	Units	£		Units	£
Process 8	870	30,450	To scrap	870	1,740
			(at sale value)		
			P&L		28,710
	870	30,450		870	30,450

Scrap (losses) account

	Units	£		Units	£
Process 8	2,250	4,500			
A/L	870	1,740	Stock c/f	3,120	6,240
	3,120	6,240		3,120	6,240
Stock b/f	3,120	6,240			

2.9 (a)

1 Total units

Opening stocks	1,200
Litres transferred in (5,000 + 1,200 + 3,000)	9,200
	10,400
Closing stock	(1,450)
N/L (10% × 9,200)	(920)
By-product Z (5% × 9,200)	(460)
Good output	(7,850)
Abnormal Gain	280

2 Equivalent units

Units	Total	Previous process XP1	Materials added P2A + P2B	Conversion
Opening stocks − to finish	1,200	–	–	720
Started + finished (7,850 − 1,200)	6,650	6,650	6,650	6,650
N/L	920	–	–	–
By-product Z	460	–	–	–
Abnormal gain	(280)	(280)	(280)	(280)
Closing stock started	1,450	1,450	1,450	435
Totals	10,400	7,820	7,820	7,525

3 Cost per unit

	$	$	$
Costs for month	15,679	10,500	22,800
Sale of Z	(920)*		
Totals	14,759	10,500	22,800
Cost per unit	1.887	1.343	3.030

Total $6.260

* This could be set against materials added.

4 Valuations

	Units	Cost ($)	Total ($)
Good Output			
Opening stock b/f	1,200		7,640
Opening stock − finish	720	3.030	2,182
Started + finished	6,650	6.260	41,629
			51,451
Abnormal gain	280	6.260	1,753
Closing stock	1,450	1.887	2,736
	1,450	1.343	1,947
	435	3.030	1,318
			6,001

5   T account

Process account

	Units	$		Units	$
Opening stock b/f	1,200	7,640			
Previous process	9,200	15,679	Good output	7,850	51,451
Material added		10,500	N/L (sale value)	920	–
Conversion costs		22,800	Z	460	920
Abnormal gain	280	1,753	Closing stock c/f	1,450	6,001
	10,680	58,372		10,680	58,372

(b)   If several products come out of a process, there are several ways that the costs could be split between them.

- *By weight or volume*. This is probably the most intuitive method but, financially, it is completely arbitrary. A bulky, low value product, will have a lot of cost apportioned to it creating an artificial loss. The product then looks as if it should be discarded.

- *By sales value*. High value products will now have a lot of costs apportioned to them, this is reasonable but can still lead to products reporting a loss where they have significant specific costs. For example, further processing costs or selling costs.

- *By net realisable value*. Generally considered the best method, it apportions costs in terms of the contribution made to joint process costs. Artificial losses are not then usually created.

- *No apportionment*. The most straightforward approach, it avoids the arbitrariness of the other methods but significantly understates the cost of products.

3

Recent Developments
in Production

Recent Developments in Production

3

 JIT

Producing items for immediate despatch to customer rather than for stock.

Often referred to as "demand–pull" production: demand from the customer activates the process.

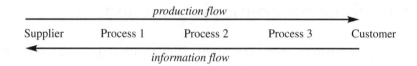

Advantages

- Focus on customer
- Reduced holding costs
- Elimination of non-value-adding activity (stockholding)
- Emphasis on quality.

Disadvantages and requirements

- Expensive to implement
- Need predictable customers
- Need reliable suppliers
- Dependent on scheduling tools
- Zero defects approach.

 TQM

Aim: to continuously improve quality.

Quality is as defined by the customer.

A company should avoid defects rather than correct them.

Costs are categorised into four types:

1 *Prevention costs.* Ensuring failures do not happen (e.g. staff training, better quality materials).
2 *Appraisal costs.* Checking for failures (e.g. quality testing, discarding tested items).
3 *Internal failure costs.* Cost of defects discovered in the company (e.g. repair costs, scrapping costs).
4 *External failure costs.* Cost of defects discovered by the customer (e.g. replacement cost, loss of goodwill).

Approach

Decisions regarding quality are traditionally made by comparing the cost of improvement with the benefits of improved quality, using the above categories.

Unfortunately, external failure costs (especially loss of goodwill) can be hard to quantify, so many TQM companies simply assume that improved quality is always worth pursuing.

🔑 MRP (materials requirements planning)

Materials scheduling software specifying material requirements and routings based on required outputs, stock policy and lead times.

🔑 MRP2 (manufacturing resource planning)

Extending MRP to staff and equipment scheduling, with particular focus on capacity levels.

🔑 ERP (enterprise resource planning)

This comprises a commercial software package that promises the seamless integration of all the information flowing through the company – financial, accounting, human resources, supply chain and customer information.

Benefits

- On-line/real-time information throughout all the functional areas of an organisation
- Data standardisation and accuracy across the enterprise
- "Best-practices" included in the applications
- The efficiency they force an organisation to undertake
- The analysis and reporting that can be used for long-term planning.

? **Questions**

3.1 Which of the following costs are likely to be reduced on the introduction of a JIT system in a company?

  (i)   Purchasing costs
  (ii) Stockholding costs
  (iii) Ordering costs
  (iv) Information system costs

  A   (i) and (ii)
  B   (ii) and (iii)
  C   (iii) and (iv)
  D   (ii) only

(2 marks)

3.2 Which of the following characteristics of a company's production system is most likely to act as an impediment to the introduction of a JIT system?

  A   The company has a range of products which it makes to the customer's specification.
  B   The company has a defect rate which varies unpredictably from period to period.
  C   The company has a very high proportion of variable labour costs in its production process.
  D   The company has a management information system that schedules production based on demand for final products.

(2 marks)

3.3 Which of the following is not suitable for a JIT production system?

  A   Batch production
  B   Jobbing production
  C   Process production
  D   Service production

(2 marks)

3.4 Which one of the following categories of cost is not usually identified as part of a TQM approach?

  A   Discretionary costs
  B   Failure costs
  C   Appraisal costs
  D   Prevention costs

(2 marks)

3.5 Which of the following statements relating to JIT and TQM approaches is most closely related to the truth?

  A   TQM and JIT are not very compatible approaches since their focus is different: one focuses on quality and the other on stock levels.
  B   TQM and JIT are not usually seen together since TQM is used by service companies and JIT by manufacturing companies.
  C   TQM and JIT are very compatible approaches as they are both largely focused on customer satisfaction.
  D   TQM and JIT are not compatible approaches since TQM requires there to be stocks so that quality checking can take place.

(2 marks)

3.6 Companies that embrace TQM often split their costs into four categories: prevention costs, appraisal costs, internal failure costs and external failure costs.

A company wants to categorise the following costs.

(i) Repair of a defective item found in work in progress.
(ii) Replacement, from stock, of previously sold goods that were returned.
(iii) Increasing the frequency of assembly machinery maintenance.
(iv) Testing the strength of a sample of output until it fails.

Which categories best reflect the nature of the above costs?

	Prevention costs	Appraisal costs	Internal failure costs	External failure costs
A	(i)	(ii)	(iii)	(iv)
B	(ii)	(i)	(iv)	(iii)
C	(i)	(iii)	(iv)	(ii)
D	(iii)	(iv)	(i)	(ii)

(2 marks)

3.7 Traditional approaches to quality are often criticised by advocates of TQM.

Which of the following are potentially valid criticisms of traditional approaches compared with TQM?

(i) Traditional systems accept a certain level of failure, whilst TQM encourages continuous improvement.
(ii) Traditional systems are focused on the company whilst TQM is customer focused.
(iii) TQM takes a much wider view of the costs of failure than the traditional approach.

A (i) and (ii) only
B (ii) and (iii) only
C (i) and (iii) only
D all of them

(2 marks)

3.8 Explain MRP, MRP2, OPT and JIT.

(5 marks)

3.9 What are the claimed advantages for a JIT system?

(5 marks)

3.10 What factors may make a JIT system inappropriate for a company?

(5 marks)

3.11 What are the characteristics of a TQM company?

(5 marks)

3.12 Specify five principles associated with synchronous manufacturing.

(5 marks)

3.13 SG plc is a long-established food manufacturer which produces semi-processed foods for fast-food outlets. While for a number of years it has recognised the need to produce good quality products for its customers, it does not have a formalised quality management programme.

A director of the company has recently returned from a conference, where one of the speakers introduced the concept of TQM and the need to recognise and classify quality costs.

Requirements

(a) Explain what is meant by TQM, and use examples to show how it may be introduced into different areas of SG plc's food production business.

(7 marks)

(b) Explain why the adoption of TQM is particularly important within a JIT production environment.

(5 marks)

(c) Explain four quality cost classifications, using examples relevant to the business of SG plc.

(8 marks)
(Total = 20 marks)

3.14 SW Ltd is a member of the SWAL group of companies. SW Ltd manufactures cleaning liquid using chemicals that it buys from a number of different suppliers. In the past, SW Ltd has used a periodic review stock control system with maximum, minimum and re-order levels to control the purchase of the chemicals and the economic order quantity model to minimise its costs.

The Managing Director of SW Ltd is thinking about changing to the use of a JIT system.

Requirements

(a) As Management Accountant, prepare a report to the Managing Director that explains how a JIT system differs from that presently being used and the extent to which its introduction would require a review of SW Ltd's quality control procedures.

(15 marks)

SW Ltd supplies its cleaning liquid to AL Ltd, another company in the SWAL group, as well as selling to its external market. SW Ltd has capacity to produce up to 500,000 litres of cleaning liquid per week. The external market demand is 350,000 litres per week, and AL Ltd demands 100,000 litres per week.

SWAL group policy

* evaluates the performance of group companies on the basis of their individual profits.
* is to set transfer prices that will encourage the maximisation of group profits.

(b) Describe how an appropriate transfer pricing policy would provide a satisfactory basis for appraising the performance of individual companies. Comment on the implications of this policy for the maximisation of group profits.

(5 marks)
(Total = 20 marks)

✓ Answers

3.1 **D**

(i) Purchasing costs will increase due to the extra requirements applied to suppliers.

(ii) Stockholding costs will reduce due to lower stock levels.

(iii) Ordering costs will increase due to the greater specification required and the increased number of small deliveries.

(iv) Information system costs will increase due to the more accurate scheduling tools required.

3.2 **B**

A Since JIT is based around satisfying customer expectations as regards both product and timing, this should pose no problems.

B The problem with unpredictable defect rates is that if the rate is unusually high at some point the defective item cannot be replaced from stock. It thus has to be started again, leading to late delivery.

C The proportion of labour costs is irrelevant.

D This is a necessity: production scheduling is often referred to as demand–pull, that is, it starts with the customer's requirements.

3.3 **A**

A Batch production uses stocks to supply customers whilst other products are being produced. Stocks are avoided in a JIT system.

B Jobbing production makes products to customer order, ideal for JIT.

C Process production produces continuous output, as long as the speed of production can be regulated this can be tailored to customer requirements.

D Services are always produced just in time as they cannot be stored.

3.4 **A**

A Discretionary costs are usually associated with zero-based budgeting: they relate to costs which the manager need not incur.

B Failure costs are usually split into internal and external components, and relate to quality failures.

C Appraisal costs are incurred in assessing whether quality targets have been reached.

D Prevention costs are those incurred whilst ensuring quality targets are reached.

3.5 **C**

A Unless there is a quality programme of some type, a company cannot afford to have low stocks in case defective items need to be replaced from stock.

B Whilst TQM can be used by service companies, it is also seen in manufacturing and other productive industries, along with JIT.

C True, customer satisfaction as regards quality and delivery times.

D A TQM system is more concerned with ensuring that errors do not occur in the first place. Any checking of items can be undertaken during the production process itself.

3.6　**D**

    (i)　This is the cost of a quality *failure discovered internally*.

    (ii)　This is the cost of a quality *failure discovered externally* (it has been returned).

    (iii)　This should help to *prevent* further failures.

    (iv)　This represents *appraising* the current production.

3.7　**D**

    (i)　Traditional systems tend to have an acceptable defect rate (e.g. a normal loss).

    (ii)　Everyone in a TQM system has a customer: a chain that leads to the ultimate customer. Traditionally acceptable defect rates are based on an assessment of the system.

    (iii)　Traditionally only internal costs are quantified, but TQM makes assumptions about external failure costs, for example, loss of goodwill.

3.8　MRP is materials requirements planning. Materials scheduling software specifying material requirements and routings based on required outputs, stock policy and lead times.

MRP2 is manufacturing resource planning. Extending MRP to staff and equipment scheduling, with particular focus on capacity levels.

OPT is optimised production technology. It is a technique which actively seeks to identify and remove – or optimise the use of – *bottleneck* resources within a manufacturing process, in order to avoid unnecessary build-ups of stock.

JIT is just in time. This is a method of production involving producing items for immediate despatch to customer rather than for stock. This is sometimes referred to as "demand–pull" production: demand from the customer activates the process.

3.9　Just-in-time systems cover purchasing, production and sales. In each case the aim is for the items involved to be completed/delivered at exactly the right moment in time for the user.

Advantages include

- a focus on value-adding activities
- a focus on the needs of the customer
- a reduction of stockholding costs
- a move away from a selling orientation towards a marketing orientation.

3.10　A JIT system has several requirements to make it function properly. If they are not present then JIT may not be appropriate.

Erratic supply of materials, for example where materials travel long distances or are supplied by unreliable companies, necessitate the holding of raw material stocks.

Unpredictable customers, perhaps the public buying on a whim, will lead to lost sales if finished good stocks are not held.

If a company has capacity constraints and its business is seasonal it will build-up its stocks in advance of the busy season.

Where a company operates a batch production system, it will produce enough output from each batch to cover demand until another batch of that product is scheduled for production.

Where a company suffers from unpredictable defect rates, it cannot replace defective production from stock and will be in danger of losing a sale.

3.11 A TQM company is characterised by the following:

Having as its clear aim the continuous improvement of quality.

Quality is as defined by the customer and is related to the concept of fitness for purpose.

The recognition that everyone has a customer.

The company will seek to avoid defects rather than correct them.

The taking of responsibility away from the quality control department and attributing it to the staff who actually produce.

3.12

1 Do not focus on balancing capacities, focus on synchronising the flow.
2 The marginal value of time at a bottleneck resource is equal to the throughput rate of the products processed by the bottleneck.
3 The marginal value of time at a non-bottleneck resource is negligible.
4 The level of utilisation of a non-bottleneck resource is controlled by other constraints within the system.
5 Resources must be utilised, not simply activated.
6 A transfer batch may not, and many times should not, be equal to the process batch.
7 A process batch should be variable both along its route and over time.

(*All seven principles are given here, only five are required.*)

3.13 (a) Total quality management may be defined as the continuous improvement in quality, productivity and effectiveness obtained by establishing responsibility for process as well as output.

It can be seen here that the essence of TQM is the establishing of responsibility for quality throughout the process. This is often expressed as the idea that everyone has a customer.

Total quality management reinforces the idea that quality is customer defined and linked to the concept of fitness for purpose. It also espouses continuous improvements and zero defects.

SG should start with a focus on its final customers: how do they define quality? With food it will clearly include not only fitness for human consumption, but also aspects such as texture, colour, additive levels and wider issues such as delivery times and packaging.

The values obtained from this would be fed back through the system: performance targets of each stage would include required quality standards of the next stage. It is to be emphasised that these are not standards imposed from outside, but rather instigated by processing staff themselves in consultation with their "customers" and management.

SG should instigate some system for monitoring existing quality and considering improvements, again this should be participative. Quality circles are one way of doing this.

SG would want to extend the TQM philosophy to other areas of its business, one area that would need to be brought in from the start would be purchasing. SG would need to consult with its suppliers and establish procedures that improve quality on a continuous basis.

(b) Just in time is defined as a system whose objective is to produce or procure products or components as they are required by a customer or for use, rather than for stock.

It is often referred to a demand–pull manufacturing as opposed to demand–push. This reflects the fact that it is the customer that triggers the production, rather than just producing in the hope of an eventual sale.

A consequence of JIT is that every item in a production system (the work in progress) is destined for a particular customer at a particular time, there is no slack and no pause.

Any item found to be defective cannot be replaced from stock (as in traditional systems) but must be remanufactured. It is now unlikely to be complete in time for delivery to customer.

Although TQM is not the only approach to quality, it does attempt to deliver zero defects which is an essential component of JIT.

(c) The main four quality cost classifications in TQM are

1 *Prevention costs.* These are costs incurred in ensuring failures do not happen. Examples include staff training and better quality materials from SG's suppliers.
2 *Appraisal costs.* Testing to discover whether failures have occurred. Examples include quality testing and discarding foodstuffs that have been tested.
3 *Internal failure costs.* These are costs of any defects discovered in the company. These would include the cost of discarding any inedible products as well as repairs where possible, such as using stickers on packaging where nutritional information has been omitted.
4 *External failure costs.* These represent the cost of any defects discovered by the customer. Note that the customers are fast-food chains, so this would include the cost of replacing any low-quality output as well as the lost goodwill.

3.14 (a)

REPORT

To: Managing Director

From: Management Accountant

Date: 21 November 2001

Subject: JIT System

Introduction
Further to our brief meeting, I set out below the features of a JIT system and the effects of its introduction.

Findings
The present stock control system is based upon the analysis of past stock movement data to establish the likely pattern of usage in the future. The use of the three control levels for maximum, minimum and reorder levels together with the economic order quantity model provides a mechanism for reviewing and controlling the levels of stock.

The present system ensures that there is a level of stock of each chemical that is held as a minimum stock. This provides SW Ltd with a safety net should there be any difficulties in obtaining the replacement supplies of chemicals, or if there is a sudden increase in the usage of a particular chemical that had not been foreseen. The problem with the system is that it assumes that past data is a reliable predictor of future requirements and this is not always true. Hence the need for the safety stock.

Just-in-time system is based on the principle that stock is received just as it is required by production, and therefore there is no safety stock. It means that as there is no stock held, there is a significant reduction in costs in terms of storage space and other stock-related costs such as insurance. However, to be able to achieve the goal of zero stock levels, there must be knowledge of the chemical requirements and this must be communicated to the suppliers so that they may structure their production and deliveries accordingly.

Quality becomes a much more significant issue when a JIT system is being used. There are two areas to consider: the quality of the chemicals that are received, and the quality of the production facility in the use of those chemicals.

The chemicals that are received must be of acceptable quality when they are received, because if they are not there is no safety stock available. As a consequence, the cleaning material production facility will be stopped until replacement chemicals are received. This would incur large costs and would not be acceptable. There needs to be a quality control check on the incoming chemicals, but this may be considered to be too late if it is done when they arrive.

An alternative is to test their quality before the supplier dispatches them, and this may have to be a condition of the supplier's contract. Ideally, both SW Ltd and its suppliers will build quality into their production systems rather than relying on inspecting poor quality out of the system at a post-production stage.

A further issue concerns the usage of the chemicals. If there are faults within the conversion process that lead to the produced cleaning material being unsatisfactory, or if there is a spillage or other loss of the chemicals in processing, there is no safety stock of chemicals that can be used. Thus, it is important to encourage an atmosphere of quality throughout the production process from handling of the chemicals, through their processing and eventual packaging for distribution to customers. There may need to be quality control checks at various stages of the process too, but since a JIT system copes very badly with the rectification of problems, the emphasis will be very much on minimising the need for such checks.

Conclusion
While there are potential cost savings through the use of a JIT system, there are many issues that need to be considered. I should be pleased to discuss this with you further if you wish.

Signed: Management Accountant.

(b) The Group transfer pricing policy is to set a transfer price that will encourage the maximisation of group profits. This is achieved by considering the opportunity costs associated with the internal sale.

At present, the cleaning material demanded by AL Ltd of 100,000 litres per week can be produced without any effect on our ability to produce the 350,000 litres per week that are demanded by our external customers. Indeed, we can produce up to a total of 500,000 litres per week within our existing capacity. This means that the internal sale to AL Ltd does not cause us to lose contribution from our external market. Therefore there is no external opportunity cost involved. This means that the present transfer price should be set at the variable cost of manufacture, adjusting, if necessary, for any variable costs that are only incurred in respect of external sales (such as packaging and distribution).

However, such a policy means that the supplier makes no profit on the internal sale. Thus, there is no incentive for the supplier to make the internal sale, particularly as performance is being measured on the basis of individual company profit.

It may be prudent, therefore, to add a small mark up to the transfer price. If this is done then care must be taken to ensure that the transfer price does not exceed any external supplier for AL, otherwise AL will source all its requirements externally.

4

Costing and Performance in the Modern Environment

Costing and Performance in the Modern Environment

4

The modern environment

Characteristics

- Highly competitive
- Competition on more than price (e.g. quality)
- Short product life cycles
- Large proportion of costs in the early stages
- Technological improvements
- Preponderance of fixed costs
- Rapid, unpredictable change.

Activity-based costing (ABC)

A form of absorption costing that tries to establish the links between costs and units by examining the activities that cause those costs.

Steps

1 Identify the activities that cause costs (cost drivers).
2 Collect costs around the drivers (cost pools).
3 Calculate the level of each activity.
4 Calculate a rate for each activity.
5 Allocate the costs to products.

Advantages

- Costs reflect complexity and diversity of production
- Selling prices more realistically reflect resources used by products
- Aids control
- Allocates responsibility
- Reduces arbitrary nature of cost absorption.

Disadvantages

- Complexity
- Still not "correct" cost per unit
- Not all costs have obvious drivers
- Implies more control than really exists
- Profits are still distorted by stock building.

Throughput accounting (TA)

Based on the "theory of constraints", throughput accounting is a method of assessing performance which is most appropriate when a company faces production constraints (often referred to as bottlenecks).

It is used to try to maximise the rate at which a company can generate profits. It does this by focusing on maximising throughput, minimising stock and controlling costs.

Throughput contribution = sales revenue − material costs.

Note that only material costs are considered variable in the short term.

Key measures

$$\text{Return per hour on bottleneck} = \frac{\text{throughput contribution}}{\text{hours on bottleneck}}$$

TA ratio = Throughput contribution in period/Conversion costs in period where conversion costs are labour and overhead.

Note: The TA ratio is often calculated as:

$$\frac{\text{throughput per hour}}{\text{conversion costs per hour}},$$

which gives the same result.

This ratio must be greater than one for the organisation to be profitable.

Backflush accounting

A simplified double entry system for production costs which is suitable for JIT and TQM systems.

Based on "trigger points", actions that trigger a double entry.

A three trigger point system would record the purchase of materials, *not* the movement or processing of materials, just their completion and sale.

Purchases

Dr Raw materials and in-process account
Cr Creditors/cash

Issue to production/movements between processes – no entries.

Items completed

Dr Finished goods account
Cr Raw materials and in-process account
— with standard material cost of completed items.

Dr Finished goods account
Cr Labour
— with standard labour cost of completed items.

Similarly with overheads.

Items sold – normal entries

The big advantage is the simplicity of the system and its associated cost saving.

The disadvantages are the loss of information regarding stocks and losses – this is considered a small cost in JIT and TQM environments.

? Questions

4.1 Which of the following statements is not true of throughput accounting?

   A Throughput accounting considers that the only variable costs in the short run are materials and components.

   B Throughput accounting considers that time at a bottleneck resource has value, not elsewhere.

   C Throughput accounting views stock building as a non-value-adding activity, and therefore discourages it.

   D Throughput accounting was designed as a decision-making tool for situations where there is a bottleneck in the production process.

(2 marks)

4.2 Which of the following is a definition of the throughput accounting ratio?

   A Throughput contribution ÷ hours on bottleneck

   B Conversion costs per hour ÷ throughput per hour

    C   Throughput per hour ÷ conversion costs per hour

    D   Total conversion costs ÷ total throughput

(2 marks)

4.3   A company is changing its costing system from traditional absorption costing (AC) based on labour hours to ABC.

It has overheads of £156,000 which are related to taking material deliveries.

The delivery information about each product is below.

Product:	X	Y	Z
Total units required	1,000	2,000	3,000
Delivery size	200	400	1,000

Total labour costs are £360,000 for 45,000 hours. Each unit of each product takes the same number of direct hours.

Assuming that the company uses the number of deliveries as its cost driver, calculate the increase or decrease in unit costs for Z arising from the change from AC to ABC.

    A   £0.50 increase

    B   £0.50 decrease

    C   £22.00 increase

    D   £22.00 decrease

(3 marks)

4.4   The following statements all concern Backflush accounting.

    (i)   Backflush accounting is good at identifying abnormal losses in a system.

    (ii) Backflush accounting is primarily a recording system used as part of double entry.

    (iii) Backflush accounting is well suited for use in JIT systems.

Which of these statements are substantially true?

    A   (i) and (ii) only

    B   (ii) and (iii) only

    C   (i) and (iii) only

    D   all of them

(2 marks)

4.5   A company uses activity-based costing to calculate the unit cost of its products. The figures for Period 3 are below.

Production set-up costs are £84,000.
Total production is 40,000 units of each of products A and B.
Each run is 2,000 units of A or 5,000 units of B.

What is the set-up cost per unit of B?

    A   £0.30

    B   £0.60

    C   £1.05

    D   £12.00

(2 marks)

4.6 Calculate the throughput accounting ratio for the following product.

Units produced		500
Time taken		200 hours
Maximum time available		200 hours
Materials purchased	1,000 kg costing	£3,000
Materials used		800 kg
Labour costs		£2,000
Overheads		£1,500
Sales		£9,000

A 1.7
B 1.9
C 2.7
D 3.1

(2 marks)

4.7 A company has recently adopted throughput accounting as a performance measuring tool. Its results for the last month are shown below.

Units produced		1,150
Units sold		800
Materials purchased	900 kg costing	£13,000
Opening material stock used	450 kg costing	£7,250
Labour costs		£6,900
Overheads		£4,650
Sales price		£35

There were no opening stocks of finished goods or closing stocks of materials.

Which of the following is closest to the throughput accounting ratio for this product?

A 0.7
B 1.2
C 1.3
D 1.7

(3 marks)

4.8 DRP Ltd has recently introduced an ABC system. It manufactures three products, details of which are set out below:

Product:	D	R	P
Budgeted annual production (units)	100,000	100,000	50,000
Batch size (units)	100	50	25
Machine set-ups per batch	3	4	6
Purchase orders per batch	2	1	1
Processing time per unit (minutes)	2	3	3

Three cost pools have been identified. Their budgeted costs for the year ending 30 June 2003 are as follows:

Machine set-up costs £150,000
Purchasing of materials £70,000
Processing £80,000.

The budgeted machine set-up cost per unit of product R is nearest to

A   £0.52
B   £0.60
C   £6.52
D   £26.09

(3 marks)

4.9   A company makes products A and B. It is experimenting with ABC.

Production set-up costs are £12,000.
Total production will be 20,000 units of each of products A and B.
Each run is 1,000 units of A or 5,000 units of B.

What is the set-up cost per unit of A, using ABC?

A   £0.30
B   £0.50
C   £0.60
D   £1.00

(2 marks)

4.10   Factory 17 has had the following results.

	Jan		Feb	
	£	£	£	£
Sales		8,600		8,600
COS				
Opening stock	900		360	
Material	2,400		2,700	
Labour	1,600		1,800	
Overheads	3,200		3,200	
	8,100		8,060	
Closing stock	360		560	
		7,740		7,500
Profit		860		1,100

Use the TA ratio to assess whether performance has improved.
Comment on the result.

(5 marks)

4.11   What is backflush accounting and what are its limitations?

(5 marks)

4.12   What are the aims of throughput accounting and what are its limitations?

(5 marks)

4.13   Which changes in the modern business environment have led to the need for ABC to replace more traditional approaches?

(5 marks)

4.14   Exe plc is a motor car manufacturer. Exe plc has been in business for many years, and it has recently invested heavily in automated processes. It continues to use a total costing system for pricing, based on recovering overheads by a labour hour absorption rate.

Exe plc is currently experiencing difficulties in maintaining its market share. It is therefore considering various options to improve the quality of its motor cars, and the quality of its service to its customers. It is also investigating its present pricing policy, which is based on the costs attributed to each motor car.

Requirements

(a) Discuss the significance to Exe plc of developing and maintaining communication links with suppliers and customers.

(10 marks)

(b) Explain the benefits (or otherwise) that an ABC system would give Exe plc.

(10 marks)

(Total = 20 marks)

4.15 X plc manufactures three products in a modern manufacturing plant, using cell operations. Budgeted output for April 2001 was

Product R 1,800 units in 36 batches
Product S 1,000 units in 10 batches
Product T 1,000 units in 40 batches

The product details are as follows:

Product:	*R*	*S*	*T*
Standard labour hours per batch	25	30	15
Batch size (units)	50	100	25
Machine set-ups per batch	3	2	5
Power (kJ) per batch	1.4	1.7	0.8
Purchase orders per batch	5	3	7
Machine hours per batch	10	7.5	12.5

During April 2001, the actual output was

Product R 1,500 units in 30 batches
Product S 1,200 units in 12 batches
Product T 1,000 units in 40 batches

The following production overhead budgetary control statement has been prepared for April 2001 on the basis that the variable production overhead varies in relation to standard labour hours produced.

Production overhead budgetary control report April 2001

	Original budget	*Flexed budget*	*Actual*	*Variances*
Output (standard hours produced)	1,800	1,710	1,710	
	£'000	£'000	£'000	£'000
Power	1,250	1,220	1,295	75 (A)
Stores	1,850	1,800	1,915	115 (A)
Maintenance	2,100	2,020	2,100	80 (A)
Machinery cleaning	800	760	870	110 (A)
Indirect labour	1,460	1,387	1,510	123 (A)
	7,460	7,187	7,690	503 (A)

After the above report had been produced, investigations revealed that every one of the individual costs could be classified as wholly variable in relation to the appropriate cost drivers.

Requirements

(a) Explain the factors that should be considered when selecting a cost driver.

(4 marks)

(b) (i) Calculate the budgeted cost per driver for each of the overhead costs.

(10 marks)

(ii) Prepare a production overhead budgetary control report for April 2001 using an activity-based approach.

(6 marks)

(Total = 20 marks)

4.16 Having attended a CIMA course on activity-based costing (ABC) you decide to experiment by applying the principles to the four products currently made and sold by your company. Details of the four products and relevant information are given below for one period:

Product	A	B	C	D
Output in units	120	100	80	120
Costs per unit	£	£	£	£
Direct material	40	50	30	60
Direct labour	28	21	14	21
Machine hours (per unit)	4	3	2	3

The four products are similar and are usually produced in production runs of 20 units and sold in batches of 10 units.

The production overhead is currently absorbed by using a machine hour rate, and the total of the production overhead has been analysed as follows:

	£
Machine department costs (rent, business rates, depreciation and supervision)	10,430
Set-up costs	5,250
Stores receiving	3,600
Inspection/quality control	2,100
Material handling and dispatch	4,620

You have ascertained that the 'cost drivers' to be used are as listed below for the overhead costs shown:

Cost	Cost driver
Set-up costs	Number of production runs
Stores receiving	Requisitions raised
Inspection/quality control	Number of production runs
Materials handling and dispatch	Orders executed

The number of requisitions raised on the stores was 20 for each product and the number of orders executed was 42, each order being for a batch of 10 of a product.

Requirements

(a) Calculate the total costs for each product if all overhead costs are absorbed on a machine hour basis.

(10 marks)

(b) Calculate the total cost of each product, using activity-based costing.

(10 marks)

(c) Calculate and list the unit product costs from your figures in (a) and (b) above, to show the differences and comment briefly on any conclusions which may be drawn which could have pricing and profit implications.

(10 marks)
(Total = 30 marks)

☑ **Answers**

4.1 **D**

All of these points are true, except D.

Throughput accounting was designed as a performance measurement tool, not a decision-making tool.

One of its advantages is that it will be used by managers to make decisions that have outcomes that are goal congruent with corporate aims. However, it was designed as a performance measurement tool.

4.2 **C**

Answer C is the same as total throughput ÷ total conversion costs, which is an alternative, correct, definition (which gives the same value).

Answers B and D are the same: they are the correct ratio inverted.

Answer A is often referred to as the return per hour.

4.3 **D**

It is worth noting that the labour cost is not needed here: it is a direct cost and will not change, regardless of the method used.

We will calculate the overhead cost per unit under both systems, and calculate the difference.

AC
Since the time per unit is the same for each product, the overheads per unit will also be the same

£156,000 ÷ 6,000 units = £26

(you would get the same answer using labour hours)

ABC

Number of deliveries for X (1,000 ÷ 200)	5
Number of deliveries for Y (2,000 ÷ 400)	5
Number of deliveries for Z (3,000 ÷ 1,000)	3
Total	13

Cost per delivery = £156,000 ÷ 13 = £12,000
Cost per unit of Z = £12,000 ÷ 3,000 units = £4
Decrease = £26 − £4 = £22.

4.4 B

(i) Backflush accounting makes assumptions about the relationships between inputs and outputs, that is, for a given output it will assume the inputs are standard, therefore it cannot cope with unexpected losses.
(ii) It is a double entry system with reduced stock entries.
(iii) Since there are few stock records, BA copes well with JIT.

4.5 B

We must divide the costs by the number of set-ups to enable the costs to be shared.

Cost driver = number of set-ups
Cost pool = £84,000
Total set-ups = 20 (for A) + 8 (for B) = 28
Rate = £84,000/28 = £3,000 per set-up

Cost for A = £3,000 × 20 set-ups = £60,000
        Per unit = £60,000/40,000 = £1.50

Cost for B = £3,000 × 8 set-ups = £24,000
        Per unit = £24,000/40,000 = £0.60.

4.6 A

The throughput accounting ratio is defined as throughput ÷ total factory costs (these can both be calculated per hour, but that is, more work for the same answer!).

Throughput = sales − all material costs = £9,000 − £3,000 = £6,000
(Note that we use materials purchased instead of materials used.)

Total factory costs = all other production costs = £2,000 + £1,500 = £3,500

TA ratio = £6,000 ÷ £3,500 = 1.7.

4.7 C

The throughput accounting ratio is defined as throughput ÷ total factory costs.

Throughput accounting aims to discourage stock building, so the ratios do not take account of stock movements.

Throughput = sales − all material costs = £35 × 800 − £13,000 = £15,000
(Note that we use materials purchased instead of materials used.)

Total factory costs = all other production costs = £6,900 + £4,650 = £11,550

TA ratio = £15,000 ÷ £11,550 = 1.3.

4.8 A

Make sure you followed the instructions and only calculated the *machine set-up cost per unit of R*. Much of the information was unnecessary.

Check that you understand the calculation of the total number of set-ups.

Total set-ups = Budget production ÷ batch size × set-ups per batch

D (100,000 ÷ 100 × 3)   3,000
R (100,000 ÷ 50 × 4)   8,000
P (50,000 ÷ 25 × 6)   12,000
                              23,000

Cost per set-up = £150,000 ÷ 23,000 = £6.52

Therefore cost per unit of R = £6.52 × 8,000 set-ups ÷ 100,000 units = £0.52.

4.9   **B**

You need to ensure that you understand the workings of cost drivers, as shown below.

Cost driver = number of set-ups
Cost pool = £12,000
Total set-ups = 20 (for A) + 4 (for B) = 24
Rate = £12,000/24 = £500 per set-up

Cost for A = £500 × 20 set-ups = £10,000
       Per unit = £10,000/20,000 = £0.50

Cost for B = £500 × 4 set-ups = £2,000
       Per unit = £2,000/20,000 = £0.10.

4.10

	Jan	*Feb*
Throughput	8,600 − 2,400 = 6,200	8,600 − 2,700 = 5,900
Conversion costs	1,600 + 3,200 = 4,800	1,800 + 3,200 = 5,000
TA ratio	1.29	1.18

The TA ratio has fallen (although it is still above one) indicating that the factory's performance has deteriorated.

The improved profits have come about by stock building, leading to a carry forward of costs. Stock building does not add value.

The company has increased its production in February which may be argued to be beneficial, but only if one of the components of production was the bottleneck. Even in this case there needs to be an effort to boost sales as this is now the major constraint on throughput.

This analysis presupposes that the company does not have a good reason for stock building, for example, an expected seasonal sales peak in excess of production capacity.

4.11   Backflush accounting is a recording process used in manufacturing businesses (and similar) to record stocks and work in progress in the company. It forms part of the company's double entry system.

The double entries are made when stocks reach "trigger points" in the process.

The main limitations of this are as follow:

Since entries are made at standard, it will fail to highlight any unexpected losses until a stock take is made. Backflush accounting is therefore most suitable in a TQM environment.

No record is kept of work in progress, leading to stocks being understated. This is not usually significant if the company operates a JIT system.

Records are not up to date – stock is not recorded as leaving an area until it has reached the end of the process.

4.12 Throughput accounting was developed to help managers improve the overall profitability of the firm.

It focuses attention on constraints or bottlenecks within the organisation which hinder production. This main concept is to maximise the rate of manufacturing output, that is, the throughput of the organisation.

Throughput accounting is only appropriate where there are constraints on production, a company with spare capacity would find traditional techniques more appropriate.

Throughput accounting is not so well understandable as more traditional techniques.

Throughput accounting assumes that all factory costs are fixed, whilst this may be true for many of these costs, it is not true for, say, overtime costs.

4.13 Recent changes necessitating ABC include

- a proportionate increase in fixed costs making the sharing of them more significant
- the increase of flexibility and diversity, leading to extra costs associated with these factors
- increasing customer focus, leading to a wider variety of products
- increased competition, leading to the need for more realistic cost information
- the increased desire to control production systems, requiring information about what activities cause which costs.

4.14 (a) The reasons for developing and maintaining communication links with suppliers and customers are many and varied. Five are considered below.

1 *Corporate growth.* Many companies have growth as one of their corporate objectives, often it is an integral part of achieving the profit targets that have been set. Exe plc cannot grow unless it starts to meet the needs of its customers and thus it needs to communicate with them to understand their needs and to ascertain why its market share is falling.

Approaches such as the balanced scorecard highlight the importance of the customer perspective.

2 *Costs.* Exe will have very high fixed costs due to the nature of its process (heavily automated). If volumes are below capacity this will lead to high overheads per unit. This can lead to a vicious spiral: high costs lead to high prices which lead to falling volumes leading to even higher unit costs. The only way to break out of this is to meet customer needs and increase volume. Proper communication is vital to this.

Marginal costing may appear to alleviate this but it does not solve the basic premise that high fixed cost companies require high sales.

3 *Budgeting.* A company starts to budget by identifying and anticipating the principal budget factor. For Exe this is clearly sales. Links with customers will help to identify probable sales levels in the future. This will help with capacity planning, sourcing of resources and staffing levels.

4 *Stock management.* Whether or not Exe adopts a JIT approach to production it will be looking to keep stocks at a reasonably low level: excessive stocks tie up capital, make profits look artificially high (especially with absorption costing valuations) and encourage staff to sell what is in stock rather than discover customers' needs and supply them.

Good stock control requires very good communication links with both suppliers and customers to properly maximise throughput.

5 *Quality.* Quality is one of the key selling points of many businesses and Exe is clearly no exception. Quality is customer defined and significantly influenced by suppliers. The introduction of a formal TQM system would reinforce the importance of quality and customer focus, but even without this Exe would get many of the benefits of customer focus.

(b) An ABC system is a form of absorption costing that dispenses with the arbitrary labour hours (or similar) as a basis for absorption and replaces it with a more realistic system based on the activities that cause the costs.

The benefits of this to Exe are set out below.

The cost split between products should be more realistic, helping to inform Exe's management as to which products are using more of the company's productive resources.

An understanding of the activities that cause costs should help the management of Exe to exercise better control over those activities, and hence the costs.

Selling prices based on cost will now more realistically reflect the resources that went into producing the car being sold, helping to ensure that Exe becomes (more) profitable.

The adoption of ABC can be part of a wider scheme encouraging everyone to focus on their customer, as required by TQM and similar approaches. It is clear that sales staff have customers, but it should also be apparent that the management accountant has customers: managers. Managers need accurate reliable relevant information to help them fulfil their roles; ABC should help provide this.

An ABC system will reflect the change in the nature of production: traditional manufacturing had a large direct labour component, and thus using labour hours to absorb overheads was realistic; a change to ABC will reinforce to management the changes in the company.

As car production becomes more customer focused and customers demand ever more personalised products, the complexity and diversity inherent in the system will be captured by the costing information.

Unfortunately ABC suffers from some drawbacks.

It implies more than it can deliver: ABC is still somewhat arbitrary. Managers may feel that this is the "correct" cost and make incorrect decisions because of this.

Activity-based costing is more complex and time-consuming than traditional approaches. It is not clear that its benefits are sufficiently high to ensure that it covers its own costs.

On balance an ABC system will probably benefit the company, but it would become much more powerful if combined with JIT and TQM production systems.

4.15 (a) The main factor to be considered when selecting a cost driver should be that there is a cause and effect relationship between the cost driver and the costs. Such a relationship may exist because of

- physical relationship
- contractual arrangements
- implicit logic.

It is necessary to consider the correlation between the cost and the proposed cost driver, while recognising that they may both be influenced by a third, as yet unknown, factor.

(b) Each of the separate costs are assumed to be associated with cost drivers as follows:

Power	–	power per batch
Stores	–	purchase orders per batch
Maintenance	–	machine hours per batch
Machinery cleaning	–	machine set-ups per batch
Indirect labour	–	standard labour hours per unit

(i) Using the original budget data to set cost driver rates

Power

	kJ
R (1.4 kJ per batch × 36 batches)	50.4
S (1.7 kJ per batch × 10 batches)	17.0
T (0.8 kJ per batch × 40 batches)	32.0
	99.4

$$\text{Cost driver rate} = \frac{\pounds1,250}{99.4 \text{ kJ}} = \pounds12.5754/\text{kJ}$$

Stores

	Orders
R (5 orders per batch × 36 batches)	180
S (3 orders per batch × 10 batches)	30
T (7 orders per batch × 40 batches)	280
	490

$$\text{Cost driver rate} = \frac{\pounds1,850}{490 \text{ orders}} = \pounds3.7755 \text{ per purchase order}$$

Maintenance

	Machine hours
R (10.0 m/c hours per batch × 36 batches)	360
S (7.5 m/c hours per batch × 10 batches)	75
T (12.5 m/c hours per batch × 40 batches)	500
	935

$$\text{Cost driver rate} = \frac{\pounds2,100}{935 \text{ m/c hours}} = \pounds2.246 \text{ per m/c hour}$$

Machinery cleaning

	Set-ups
R (3 set-ups per batch × 36 batches)	108
S (2 set-ups per batch × 10 batches)	20
T (5 set-ups per batch × 40 batches)	200
	328

$$\text{Cost driver rate} = \frac{\pounds800}{328 \text{ set-ups}} = \pounds2.439 \text{ per set-up}$$

Calculation of the standard number of cost drivers for the actual output

	R	S	T	Total
Power	(1.4 × 30)	(1.7 × 12)	(0.8 × 40)	94.4 kJ
Stores	(5 × 30)	(3 × 12)	(7 × 40)	466 purchase orders
Maintenance	(10 × 30)	(7.5 × 12)	(12.5 × 40)	890 machine hours
Machinery cleaning	(3 × 30)	(2 × 12)	(5 × 40)	314 machine set-ups
Indirect labour (as per question)				

Flexed budget

Cost based on activity	£
Power (£12.5754 × 94.4)	1,187
Stores (£3.7755 × 466)	1,759
Maintenance (£2.246 × 890)	1,999
Machinery cleaning (£2.439 × 314)	766
Indirect labour (as per question)	1,387

(ii)

Production overhead budgetary control report – April 2001

	Original budget	Flexed budget	Actual	Variance
	£'000	£'000	£'000	£'000
Power	1,250	1,187	1,295	108 (A)
Stores	1,850	1,759	1,915	156 (A)
Maintenance	2,100	1,999	2,100	101 (A)
Machinery cleaning	800	766	870	104 (A)
Indirect labour	1,460	1,387	1,510	123 (A)
	7,460	7,098	7,690	592 (A)

4.16 (a) Overheads absorbed on machine hour basis

Machine hour absorption rate = Total overheads/Total machine hours

$$= \frac{£10,400 + £5,520 + £3,600 + £2,100 + £4,620}{(120 \times 4) + (100 \times 3) + (80 \times 2) + (120 \times 3)}$$

$$\frac{£26,000}{1,300} = £20 \text{ per machine hour}$$

Total costs based on machine hour basis

	A	B	C	D
	£	£	£	£
Direct materials	40	50	30	60
Direct labour	28	21	14	21
Production overhead	80	60	40	60
Production cost/unit	148	131	84	141
Output in units	120	100	80	120
Total production cost	£17,760	£13,100	£6,720	£16,920

(b) Overheads absorbed based on ABC

	£	Overhead costs Level of activity	Cost/activity
Machine department cost	10,430	1,300	£8.02/hour
Set-up costs	5,250	21*	£250.00/run
Stores receiving costs	3,600	80**	£45.00/requisition
Inspection/quality costs	2,100	21*	£100.00/run
Material handling and despatch	4,620	42	£110.00/order

Workings

*No of production runs = output in units/20

$$= \frac{120 + 100 + 80 + 120}{20}$$

$$= \frac{420}{20} = 21$$

**No of requisition raised = No. of products × 20
= 4 × 20 = 80

Total costs based on ABC

	A £	B £	C £	D £
Direct materials	40.00	50.00	30.00	60.00
Direct labour	28.00	21.00	14.00	21.00
Machine dept costs	32.09	24.07	16.05	24.07
Set-up costs	12.50	12.50	12.50	12.50
Stores receving	7.50	9.00	11.25	7.50
Inspection	5.00	5.00	5.00	5.00
Material handling	11.00	11.00	11.00	11.00
Production cost/unit	136.09	132.57	99.80	141.07
Output in units	120	100	80	120
Total production costs	£16,331	£13,257	£7,984	£16,928

(c) Comparison of the two unit costs calculated in (a) and (b) above.

Product	A £	B £	C £	D £
Based on machine hour rate	148.00	131.00	84.00	141.00
ABC method	136.09	132.57	99.80	141.07
Difference	111.91	(1.57)	(15.80)	(0.07)

Products A and C have the largest differences. The ABC approach in theory, attributes the cost of resources to each product which uses those resources on a more appropriate basis than the traditional method. The implication is that product A is more profitable than the traditional approach implies, whereas C is less profitable. If selling prices were determined on costs based on the traditional absorption method, the organisation might consider increasing the price of C and reducing that of A.

5

Standard Costing

Standard Costing 5

A **standard cost** is a unit cost prepared in advance based on expected resource usage.

Standards can be prepared on several bases.

- *Ideal standards*. Assuming 100% efficiency, no wastage and ideal performance.
- *Basic standards*. Long-run standards for situations that do not change significantly.
- *Current standards*. Based on recent operating experience.
- *Expected standards*. Based on realistic targets for performance.

The last of these is probably the most widely used.

Benefits

- Assistance to budgeting
- Detailed performance evaluation possible
- Acts as a target: motivational benefits
- Highlights controllable areas
- Aids in setting selling prices.

Behavioural implications

Standard costs will motivate best if

- They are based on controllable factors
- Staff have some say in the level of the standards (participation)
- Staff ability is taken into account
- Rewards/incentives are linked to variances
- Standards are "hard but achievable".

The nature of staff also needs to be taken into account: some staff are primarily motivated by the need to succeed, others by the need to avoid failure.

Criticisms of standard costing

The main criticisms are

- an obsession with costs; many other factors are important to corporate success
- the implication that a reduction in costs is always good; ignoring the benefits of, for example, improved quality
- the idea that there is a standard which is good enough, when many management philosophies preach continual improvement
- the inability to deal with short life cycles which lead to a marked reduction in unit costs over short-time periods
- the inability to deal with constantly changing work practices
- the inappropriateness of having a standard when products are tailored to a customer's specification.

Variance interpretation

Where the actual cost is different to standard a variance arises (calculation of these is in the next chapter).

You need to be able to suggest causes of a particular variance.

For example, an adverse raw material price variance may be due to

- unexpected inflation
- better quality materials
- failure to obtain a bulk discount
- improved quality
- rapid delivery.

Sometimes a single cause can explain two or more variances. For example, better quality materials may lead to a favourable material usage variance and an adverse price variance.

In the exam you should always try to identify any situations like this.

? Questions

5.1   The following may be claimed to be disadvantages of a standard costing system.

   (i)   A standard costing system implies that a certain level of failure is acceptable in the modern business environment, but the aim should be to continuously improve.
   (ii) A standard costing system is much too narrow in its assessment of performance. Modern systems such as the balanced scorecard are much wider in scope.
   (iii) A standard costing system is not suitable for use in a responsibility accounting system as the standards tend to be imposed from above rather than being set by the manager.

Which of these criticisms have reasonable validity?

A   (i) and (ii) only
B   (ii) and (iii) only
C   (i) and (iii) only
D   all of them

(2 marks)

5.2   In standard costing there are often said to be four main types of standards: ideal standards, basic standards, current standards and expected standards.

Consider the following situations:

(i)   A bicycle manufacturer has the standard number of wheels per bicycle set at two.

(ii)   A bus company has had the standard time for a journey set at the same level for the last eight years.

(iii)   A drug company has based its mix standard for a new drug on the chemical information from the research team and estimates of wastage from its production team.

(iv)   A clock manufacturer has set the standard price of its components by considering last year's prices and modifying them for anticipated inflation.

Which categorisation below is the most reasonable?

	Ideal standards	Basic standards	Current standards	Expected standards
A	(i)	(ii)	(iii)	(iv)
B	(iii)	(iv)	(ii)	(i)
C	(ii)	(iii)	(iv)	(i)
D	(i)	(ii)	(iv)	(iii)

(2 marks)

5.3   It is now Month 11 in a company's year. The company has announced that it will introduce a standard costing system from Month 1 next year.

The company will set the new year's standard (purchase) price for its components by looking at the actual price paid for Month 12 this year, and adding 8%, which is the anticipated inflation rate for next year.

The following statements have been made by managers:

(i)   Inflation is likely to make variances favourable in the first few months of the year, and adverse in the last few months of the year.

(ii)   Over the full year this will reward purchasing staff who improve on last year's overall performance, after taking account of the effects of inflation.

(iii)   Staff will try to buy components cheaply for Month 12 of this year, in preparation for the standard costing starting next year.

Which of these statements are substantially false?

A   (i) and (ii) only
B   (ii) and (iii) only
C   (i) and (iii) only
D   all of them

(2 marks)

5.4 A company has three grades of labour: they all do the same basic task, but higher grades have more experience. The company operates a standard costing system, but only calculates one rate variance and one efficiency variance for all staff together. No idle time variance is calculated.

A favourable labour efficiency variance together and a favourable labour rate variance have just occurred and several departments are claiming credit, as detailed below.

  (i)   Human resource states that a greater proportion of the staff were higher grade than was standard, this produced a better quality of work and less wastage.
  (ii) Production planning reorganised work schedules, reducing staff changeover times and requiring less of the work to be done in overtime, which is at premium rates.
  (iii) Maintenance claimed there were less machine breakdowns due to a more frequent maintenance schedule brought in as part of an ongoing aim of reducing down-time.

Which of these is the most likely explanation of the variances calculated?

A   (i) only
B   (ii) only
C   (iii) only
D   none of them

(2 marks)

5.5 A company has a favourable material usage variance.

Several reasons for this have been proposed and are shown below.

  (i)   The company has purchased higher quality materials leading to less wastage.
  (ii) The company has invested in faster equipment leading to greater throughput.
  (iii) The company has invested in staff training, leading to fewer defective units of output.

Which of these are likely explanations?

A   (i) and (ii) only
B   (ii) and (iii) only
C   (i) and (iii) only
D   all of them

(2 marks)

5.6 Suggest causes of a favourable labour efficiency variance.

Could any of these causes also be linked to an adverse material price variance?

(5 marks)

5.7 It has been said that a standard costing system is not appropriate in a TQM environment. Why should this be so?

(5 marks)

5.8 What factors should be considered when deciding whether to investigate a variance?

(5 marks)

5.9 How should inflation be dealt with in the standard-setting process?

(5 marks)

5.10 W plc provides a range of standard products to the aircraft industry. The company has a number of sites throughout the country and some of them make identical products. The sites have differently aged machinery.

For a number of years, the company has used standard costing to control its production costs. The standard costs are set centrally at head office and are imposed on the managers of the sites.

At a recent meeting of the site managers, a number of them complained that the standards imposed upon them were unfair.

Requirement

(a) Explain the reasons for and against the imposition of centrally set standard costs on site managers.

(12 marks)

The Managing Director of W plc recently attended a conference on "World Class Manufacturing" and was very interested in the developments in computer-controlled, robotic manufacturing processes.

He overheard some other delegates speaking about the relevance of standard costing in such an environment, particularly given the overriding influences of TQM.

(b) Briefly discuss the relevance of standard costing techniques in a TQM environment that uses computer-controlled, robotic manufacturing processes.

(8 marks)
(Total = 20 marks)

✅ **Answers**

5.1 **A**

   (i) Approaches such as TQM encourage continuous performance, which implies there cannot be a standard performance.
  (ii) Standard costing looks only at costs in its assessment of performance, whereas the balanced scorecard also covers areas such as innovation and learning.
 (iii) A responsibility accounting system can exist with top-down or bottom-up budgeting; it has more to do with managers controlling resources than how budgets are set.

5.2 **D**

Ideal standards: assuming 100% efficiency, no wastage and ideal performance – (i) – if the company makes 100 bicycles it will almost certainly use more than 200 wheels due to errors, defects, etc.
Basic standards: long-run standards for situations that do not change significantly – (ii) – eight years is a long term here.
Current standards: based on recent operating experience – (iv) – recent, modified performance.
Expected standards: based on realistic targets for performance – (iii) – an attempt has been made to make this realistic.

5.3 **D**

   (i) Variances are likely to be favourable all year as the actual price climbs towards the standard. Even when the actual price has reached the standard the variance will simply be nil.

   (ii) Staff will be rewarded if they do better than Month 12, this may not be typical of the year.

   (iii) Staff will be tempted to buy expensive components for Month 12 this year so that favourable variances become easier to achieve.

5.4 **D**

   (i) Higher grades are likely to be not only more efficient but also more expensive.

   (ii) The reduced changeover times will improve efficiency, and the reduced overtime will reduce the rate.

   (iii) This improves efficiency, but not rate.

5.5 **C**

   (i) Less material will be used than is standard.

   (ii) Faster equipment increases the number of units produced; there is nothing to imply that the material requirements will be anything other than proportionate.

   (iii) A lower defect rate means that less material is used for the given output than is standard.

5.6 A favourable labour efficiency variance may be due to

   • higher grade/skill labour being used
   • introduction of piece rate pay
   • new, more efficient, machinery
   • staff improvement due to learning, etc.
   • motivated, enthusiastic staff.

   If the material price variance is adverse it could be due to

   • better quality materials, higher price, less wastage.

5.7 Standard costing may not be appropriate in a TQM environment for the following reasons.

   Standard costing focuses on costs; TQM focuses on customer satisfaction.
   Standard costing assumes that a reduction in costs is always good; ignoring many of the benefits of improved quality.
   Standard costing is based on the idea that there is a standard which is good enough, whilst TQM preaches continuous improvement.
   TQM leads to short life cycles which tend to experience a marked reduction in unit costs over short time periods; standard costing needs unchanging costs.
   TQM is customer focused, which may lead to a company tailoring its products to a customer's specification – there is then no standard product.

5.8 The following factors should be considered.

   The size of the variance – large variances are more likely to be investigated than small; large may be defined as a percentage of standard.
   Adverse variances are more likely to be investigated than favourable.
   Any costs incurred in the process of investigation need to be considered.

The benefits of correction, should the system prove to be out of control.

The trend of past variances: if variances are getting progressively larger then there may well be some underlying cause which needs to be identified and controlled.

5.9   Inflation is a general rise in the level of prices. It therefore impacts on price standards, affecting measured performance.

One of the most common ways of setting standards is to base them on last year's performance. In times of inflation this would leave a standard price that was unrealistically low, leading to adverse variances.

Even then it is not clear whether the average price from last year or the final price would be used.

The, apparently, intuitive position would be to use year end prices from last year and add inflation. Unfortunately this would produce estimated year end prices for the current year with favourable variances occurring all year.

The most common approach is to estimate "mid-year" prices for the current year, either by using last year's average price and adding a full year's inflation or by using the closing price with 6 months' inflation.

This approach will tend to lead to favourable variances in the first half of the year and adverse variances in the second half. Overall, the variance should be close to zero.

General inflation can be estimated using historical trends, government targets or economists' estimates . It is worth bearing in mind that it can have "knock on" effects such as wage demands and fluctuating exchange rate.

5.10   (a)   A standard cost is a carefully predetermined unit cost which is prepared for each cost unit. It contains details of the standard amount and price of each resource that will be utilised in providing the service or manufacturing the product.

Standards assist budgeting, enable detailed performance evaluation, act as a target and can often have motivational benefits.

If standards are set centrally some of these benefits will be enhanced and others weakened.

Reasons for centrally set standards

The management should be able to better achieve goal congruence, highlighting the same areas of importance across the company.

Managers can better resist the introduction of slack which employees may use to make targets easier and performance look better.

Revision of standards only takes place in one location each year rather than at each site, reducing the effect and cost of duplication.

More senior staff are better trained and will probably have more experience than local staff, leading to more realistic targets.

Centrally set standards reduce the need for discussion with local staff, reducing the total management time spent on setting standards.

Reasons against centrally set standards

Central management should concentrate more on strategy and less on the detailed operational goals.

The situation that each location is in (e.g. costs generated by aging machines) is different, and so what may be an easy target at one location may be hard at another.

Local managers are not allowed to participate in decisions and therefore they may resent the targets set. Participation is well documented as having motivational benefits.

Giving more power to local managers will increase input from staff "at the sharp end" leading to standards that are up to date and reflect current operating conditions.

Conclusion

On balance most companies allow some participation and reduce the effect of built-in slack by ensuring that local targets are approved (and if necessary revised) before they become accepted standards. This would seem most appropriate for W plc.

(b)   There are a number of reasons why standard costing may not be appropriate in a TQM environment. These include the following.

An obsession with costs; many other factors are important to corporate success. A system that focused primarily on quality and customer satisfaction would be appropriate in a TQM environment.

The implication that a reduction in costs is always good, in fact a TQM system will almost certainly increase costs in the short run.

TQM advocates continual improvement, whilst standard costing is based on the idea that there is a standard which is good enough; they thus are philosophically different.

A standard cost is usually only revised annually, whilst TQM should lead to constantly changing work practices leaving standards out of date.

Since quality is customer defined, standard costing becomes inappropriate as each product may be tailored to a customer's specification.

Standard costing works best where costs are primarily variable, enabling them to be flexed with the activity level. In the environment specified, most costs are likely to be fixed, rendering flexing less useful.

Despite the above, standard costing is still used by some companies in this kind of environment. Reasons include the following.

Inertia: many companies have always used this type of system; it is well understood, uses existing systems and highlights the effect on profits of changes.

It is not obvious what should replace standard costing; clearly some approach which highlights quality and is flexible. Unfortunately quality certainly costs but it is hard to quantify the benefits. Fixed costs are hard to control under any system, and performance based on them is also hard to ascertain.

Some of these problems can be overcome with the use of techniques such as the balanced scorecard and activity-based budgeting (and costing).

Traditional Variance Analysis

Traditional Variance Analysis

6

> **!** A variance represents the difference between standard and actual performance. It is an important tool for performance evaluation.

π Calculation

All variances compare actual value with standard. They are based on flexed costs, that is standard costs that take account of actual activity levels. You need to know the variance formulae.

Materials price variance

Did pay	x = actual price paid
Should have paid	$\underline{x}$ = standard price paid for actual *purchases*
Variance	$\underline{\underline{x}}$

Materials usage variance

Did use	x = actual quantity used
Should have used	$\underline{x}$ = standard quantity used for *actual* production
Difference	x
At standard price	$\underline{x}$
Variance	$\underline{\underline{x}}$

Labour rate variance

Did pay	x = actual amount paid
Should have paid	$\underline{x}$ = standard amount paid for actual hours paid for
Variance	$\underline{\underline{x}}$

Labour idle time variance

Idle hours	x
At standard rate	x
Variance	x

Labour efficiency variance

Hours were	x = actual hours worked
Should have been	x = standard hours worked for *actual* production
Difference	x
At standard rate	x
Variance	x

Variable overhead rate variance

Did pay	x = actual amount paid
Should have paid	x = standard amount paid for actual hours worked
Variance	x

Variable overhead efficiency variance

Hours were	x = actual hours worked
Should have been	x = standard hours worked for *actual* production
Difference	x
At standard rate	x
Variance	x

Fixed overhead expenditure variance

Fixed overheads were	x = actual fixed overheads
Should have been	x = budget fixed overheads
Variance	x

Fixed overhead volume variance

Volume was	x = actual production in units
Should have been	x = budget production
Difference	x
At standard	x
Variance	x

Sales price variance

Revenue was	x = actual sales income
Should have been	x = standard price of actual units sold
Variance	$\underline{\underline{x}}$

Sales volume variance

Volume was	x = actual number of units sold
Should have been	x = budget number of units sold
Difference	x
At standard margin	x = profit per unit
Variance	$\underline{\underline{x}}$

An operating statement reconciles actual results to the budget.

It uses the variances calculated above.

? Questions

6.1   A company uses a standard costing system.

According to the standard cost card: 6 kg of material X is used to make 5 kg of product Y and 1 kg of X costs £8.

Actual results for Month 9 were

Output of Y	28,000 kg
Input of X	32,000 kg
Cost of X	£240,000

There were no stocks of any kind.

The material X usage variance was

A   £12,000 (F)
B   £12,800 (F)
C   £30,000 (F)
D   £32,000 (F)

(3 marks)

Use the following information to answer the next two questions.

Company Y operates a standard costing system. The following is an extract from the standard cost card of one unit of its main product.

Labour: 3 hours at £7.75/hour.

In actual fact, the company spent the following on labour:

Normal time	5,500 hours at £8.15
Overtime	1,200 hours at £12.00

Included in the normal time above are 800 hours of stoppage time due to a machine break-down. The company does *not* separately calculate idle time variances.

The company produced 2,300 units.

6.2 Which of the following is closest to the labour rate variance?

    A   £2,200 (A)
    B   £5,750 (A)
    C   £6,980 (A)
    D   £7,300 (A)

                    (2 marks)

6.3 Which of the following is closest to the labour efficiency variance?

    A   £1,550 (F)
    B   £1,550 (A)
    C   £5,750 (F)
    D   £5,750 (A)

                    (2 marks)

Use the following information to answer the next two questions.

A company makes product X in batches of three. It operates a standard costing system.

It made 840 units last month with the variable overheads costing £108,500.

Standard cost card for one batch of X:

Variable overheads 20 hours at £18.20/hour = £364 per batch

Labour hours worked were 5,900. In addition there were 30 idle hours.

6.4 Which of the following is closest to the variable overhead rate variance?

    A   £574 (A)
    B   £1,120 (A)
    C   £5,640 (A)
    D   £6,580 (A)

                    (2 marks)

6.5 Which of the following is closest to the variable overhead efficiency variance?

    A   £1,120 (A)
    B   £5,460 (A)
    C   £6,006 (A)
    D   £6,580 (A)

                    (2 marks)

Use the following information to answer the next two questions.

A company operates a standard absorption costing system.

Output was budgeted at 8,100 but was actually 8,320.

Fixed overheads were budgeted at £40,500 but were actually £42,600.

Stocks rose by 200 units during the period. There were no opening stocks.

6.6 Which of the following is closest to the fixed overhead rate (expenditure) variance?

    A £930 (A)
    B £980 (A)
    C £1,000 (A)
    D £2,100 (A)

(2 marks)

6.7 Which of the following is closest to the fixed overhead volume variance?

    A £1,000 (A)
    B £100 (F)
    C £1,100 (F)
    D £1,130 (F)

(2 marks)

Use the following information to answer the next two questions.

A company makes product X.

The company operates a standard absorption costing system.

The information below represents the performance of Month 11.

	Budget/standard	Actual
Sales	5,500 units	6,200 units
Production	5,700 units	6,300 units
Selling price	£23	£21
Cost per unit	£18	£19

6.8 Which of the following is closest to the sales price variance?

    A £3,700 (F)
    B £12,400 (A)
    C £12,600 (A)
    D £18,600 (A)

(2 marks)

6.9 Which of the following is closest to the sales margin volume variance?

    A £1,000 (F)
    B £3,500 (F)
    C £10,500 (F)
    D £11,500 (F)

(2 marks)

6.10 A company operates a standard absorption costing system.

Sales were budgeted at 450 units but were actually 480 units.

Closing stock was budgeted at 20 units but was actually 30 units.

There were no opening stocks.

Fixed overheads were budgeted at £18,330 but were actually £18,400.

Which of the following is closest to the total fixed overhead variance?

A £70 (A)

B £1,150 (F)

C £1,170 (F)

D £1,490 (F)

(3 marks)

6.11 XY plc uses a standard absorption costing system. Details for Period 5 were

	Budget	Actual
Sales units	5,600	5,940
Selling price per unit	£18.00	£18.75
Profit per unit	£4.60	£5.20

The sales price and volume variances for Period 5 were

	Price (£)	Volume (£)
A	4,455 (A)	1,564 (F)
B	4,455 (F)	1,564 (F)
C	4,455 (A)	1,768 (F)
D	4,455 (F)	1,768 (F)

(2 marks)

The following data is to be used for the subsequent two questions.

M plc sells televisions that it purchases through a regional distributor. An extract from its budget for the four-week period ended 28 October 2001 shows that it planned to sell 500 televisions at a unit price of £300, which would give a contribution to sales ratio of 30%.

Actual sales were 521 televisions at an average selling price of £287. The actual contribution to sales ratio averaged 26%.

6.12 The sales price variance (to the nearest £1) was

A £6,773 (A)

B £6,500 (A)

C £6,500 (F)

D £6,773 (F)

(2 marks)

6.13 The sales volume contribution variance (to the nearest £1) was

A £1,890 (F)

B £1,808 (F)

C £1,638 (F)

D £1,567 (F)

(2 marks)

6.14 The following data have been extracted from the budget working papers of WR Ltd:

Activity (Machine hours)	Overhead cost £
10,000	13,468
12,000	14,162
16,000	15,549
18,000	16,242

In March 2002, the actual activity was 13,780 machine hours and the actual overhead cost incurred was £14,521.

The total overhead expenditure variance is nearest to

A   £1,750 (F)
B   £250 (F)
C   £250 (A)
D   £4,520 (A)

(4 marks)

6.15   A company operates a standard costing system.

Standard cost information for one unit is as follows:

Variable overheads   4 hours at £3.50/hour

The company made 3,700 widgets last month with the variable overheads costing £53,640.

Labour hours were 14,900 worked, 15,200 paid; the difference was idle time.

Requirement

Calculate the variable overhead rate and efficiency variances.

(5 marks)

6.16   A company operates a standard costing system.

Standard cost information for one unit is as follows:

Materials   8 kg at £13.50/kg

The company budgeted to make 4,800 units last month but actually made only 4,500.

Material purchased was 39,900 kg, costing £13.70 per kg, whilst the amount used was 38,700 kg.

Calculate the material price and usage variances and suggest a cause for each of these variances.

(5 marks)

6.17   A company makes product X in batches of four. It operates a standard costing system.

Budget production last month was 924 units. The company actually made 932 units with the labour costing £107,700.

Standard cost card for one batch of X:

Labour: 46 hours at £11.50/hour = £529 per batch.

Labour hours worked were 10,320. In addition, there were 20 idle hours.

The company does *not* separately calculate an idle time variance.

Calculate the labour rate and efficiency variances.

(5 marks)

6.18   A company makes product X.

The company operates a standard absorption costing system.

Recent performance is shown below.

The standard selling price was £8 per unit but it was actually £6 per unit.
The standard cost was £5 per unit but it was actually £4 per unit.
Production was budgeted at 143 units but was actually 121 units.
Closing stock was budgeted at 22 units but was actually 28 units.
There were no opening stocks.

Calculate the sales price and sales margin volume variances. Suggest a cause for each of these variances.

(5 marks)

6.19   The standard cost card for one unit of product X.

		£
Materials	7 kg at £35.00	245.00
Labour	20 hours at £12.00	240.00
Variable overheads	20 hours at £8.00	160.00
Fixed overheads	20 hours at £15.00	300.00
		945.00
Selling price		1,500.00
Profit		555.00

The budget was for 8,800 units produced and sold.

Actual results were

		£
Sales	8,700 units	12,125,000
Produced	8,900 units	
Materials – purchased and used	62,450 kg	2,183,000
Labour – paid and worked	177,450 hours	2,246,000
Variable overheads		1,435,000
Fixed overheads		2,650,000

Requirement

Calculate the variances in as much detail as possible.
Produce an operating statement.

(20 marks)

6.20   JK plc operates a chain of fast-food restaurants. The company uses a standard marginal costing system to monitor the costs incurred in its outlets. The standard cost of one of its most popular meals is as follows:

	£ per meal
Ingredients (1.08 units)	1.18
Labour (1.5 min)	0.15
Variable conversion costs (1.5 min)	0.06
The standard selling price of this meal is	1.99

In one of its outlets, which has budgeted sales and production activity level of 50,000 such meals, the number of such meals that were produced and sold during April 2003 was 49,700.

The actual cost data was as follows:

	£
Ingredients (55,000 units)	58,450
Labour (1,200 hours)	6,800
Variable conversion costs (1,200 hours)	3,250
Actual revenue from the sale of the meals	96,480

Requirements

(a) Calculate

    (i) the total budgeted contribution for April 2003
    (ii) the total actual contribution for April 2003.

(3 marks)

(b) Present a statement that reconciles the budgeted and actual contribution for April 2003.

Show all variances to the nearest £1 and in as much detail as possible.

(17 marks)
(Total = 20 marks)

✅ Answers

6.1 **B**

The company should use 1.2 kg of X to make 1 kg of Y.

Did use	32,000 kg = actual quantity used
Should have used (28,000 × 1.2)	33,600 kg = standard quantity used for *actual* production
Difference	1,600 kg
At standard price	£8
Variance	£12,800

6.2 **D**

The actual payment for labour is

		£
Normal time	5,500 hours at £8.15	44,825
Overtime	1,200 hours at £12.00	14,400
Total	6,700 hours	59,225

This is based on hours paid so stoppage time is irrelevant.

Rate variance

	£
Did pay	59,225 = actual amount paid
Should have paid (6,700 × £7.75)	51,925 = standard amount paid for actual hours worked
Variance	7,300 (A)

6.3 **A**

Labour efficiency variance

Hours were	6,700 = actual hours worked
Should have been	6,900 = standard hours worked for
(2,300 × 3 hours)	*actual* production
Difference	200
At standard rate	£7.75
Variance	£1,550 (F)

6.4 **B**

Do not use hours paid for this calculation.

Work either in batches *or* units, be consistent: 840 units = 280 batches (3 units per batch).

Variable overhead rate variance

£

Did pay	108,500 = actual amount paid
Should have paid	107,380 = standard amount paid for actual
(5,900 × £18.20)	hours worked
Variance	1,120 (A)

6.5 **B**

Variable overhead efficiency variance

Hours were	5,900 = actual hours worked
Should have been	5,600 = standard hours worked for
(280 batches × 20 hours)	*actual* production
Difference	300
At standard rate	£18.20
Variance	£5,460 (A)

6.6 **D**

It is worth calculating the standard fixed overhead rate before you start
£40,500 ÷ 8,100 units = £5/unit

You probably spotted that the stock was irrelevant here – overheads are absorbed into production, which you are given here.

Fixed overhead expenditure variance

£

Fixed overheads were	42,600 = actual fixed overheads
Should have been	40,500 = budget fixed overheads
Variance	2,100 (A)

6.7 **C**

Fixed overhead volume variance

Volume was	8,320 = actual production in units
Should have been	8,100 = budget production
Difference	220
At standard	£5
Variance	£1,100 (F)

6.8 **B**

Don't forget that the sales price variance looks at the effect on revenue.

Sales price variance

£

Revenue was (6,200 × £21)	130,200 = actual sales income
Should have been (6,200 × £23)	142,600 = standard price of actual units sold
Variance	12,400 (A)

6.9 **B**

The sales volume variance is a margin variance: value it at standard profit per unit.

Sales volume variance

Volume was	6,200 = actual number of units sold
Should have been	5,500 = budget number of units sold
Difference	700
At standard margin	£5 = profit per unit
Variance	£3,500 (F)

6.10 **D**

Total cost variances are always calculated as flexed budget − actual; remember that this is based on production and not sales.

Budget production = 450 + 20 = 470
Actual production = 480 + 30 = 510

The standard absorption rate is £18,330 ÷ 470 = £39 per unit.

£

Flexed budget (510 × £39)	19,890
Actual	18,400
Variance	1,490 (F)

6.11 **B**

Make sure you know these standard variances.

Since sales volumes are above budget and prices have risen, both variances are favourable.

Sales price variance

£

Revenue was (5,940 × £18.75)	111,375 = actual sales income
Should have been (5,940 × £18.00)	106,920 = standard price of actual units sold
Variance	4,455 (F)

Sales volume variance

Volume was	5,940 = actual number of units sold
Should have been	5,600 = budget number of units sold
Difference	340
At standard margin	£4.60 = profit per unit
Variance	£1,564 (F)

6.12 **A**

Make sure you know these standard variances.

Be careful about the signs of these variances.

Sales price variance

£

Revenue was (521 × £287)	149,527 = actual sales income
Should have been (521 × £300)	156,300 = standard price of actual units sold
Variance	6,773 (A)

6.13 **A**

Sales volume variance

Volume was	521 = actual number of units sold
Should have been	500 = budget number of units sold
Difference	21
At standard margin (30% × £300)	£90 = profit per unit
Variance	£1,890 (F)

6.14 **B**

You need to observe that the overheads are partly fixed and partly variable.

You can spot this by quickly checking if costs have risen in line with activity (e.g. when hours rise from 10,000 to 12,000 i.e. 20%; costs rise, but by less than 20%).

Using the high/low method to split costs fixed and variable:

	Hours	£
High	18,000	16,242
Low	10,000	13,468
Difference	8,000	2,774

VC per hour = £2,774 ÷ 8,000 hours = £0.3468/hour

FC = total costs − VC = 13,468 − 0.3468 × 10,000 = £10,000

Flexed costs:
FC + VC/unit × Quantity (£10,000 + £0.3468 × 13,780)

	£
Budgeted cost	14,779
Actual costs	(14,521)
Variance	258 (F)

6.15 Do *not* use hours paid for this calculation.

Variable overhead rate variance

	£	
Did pay	53,640	= actual amount paid
Should have paid	52,150	= standard amount paid for actual
(14,900 × £3.50)		hours worked
Variance	1,490 (A)	

Variable overhead efficiency variance

Hours were	14,900	= actual hours worked
Should have been	14,800	= standard hours worked for
(3,700 × 4)		*actual* production
Difference	100	
At standard rate	£3.50	
Variance	£350 (A)	

6.16 Note that the budget information is irrelevant.

The actual amount paid was 39,900 × £13.70 = £546,630

Materials price variance

	£	
Did pay	546,630	= actual price paid
Should have paid	538,650	= standard price paid for
(39,900 × £13.50)		actual *purchases*
Variance	7,980 (A)	

Materials usage variance

Did use	38,700	= actual quantity used
Should have used	36,000	= standard quantity used for
(4,500 × 8)		*actual* production
Difference	2,700	
At standard price	£13.50	
Variance	£36,450 (A)	

A possible cause of an adverse price variance is the failure to buy in bulk leading to a loss of discounts.

The usage variance could be caused by using lower grade staff leading to more wastage.

6.17 Make sure you work either in batches *or* units; be consistent

932 units = 233 batches (4 units per batch)

Actual labour hours were 10,340, including the idle time (since idle time variance is not separately identified in this question).

As always, budget information is irrelevant.

Labour rate variance

£

Did pay	107,700 = actual amount paid
Should have paid	118,910 = standard amount paid for actual
(10,340 × £11.50)	hours worked
Variance	11,210 (F)

Labour efficiency variance

Hours were	10,340 = actual hours worked
Should have been	10,718 = standard hours worked
(233 batches × 46 hours)	for *actual* production
Difference	378
At standard rate	£11.50
Variance	£4,347 (F)

6.18 Do not forget that the sales price variance looks at the effect on revenue.

Note that actual sales = 121 − 28 = 93 units.

Sales price variance

£

Revenue was (93 × £6)	558 = actual sales income
Should have been (93 × £8)	744 = standard price of actual units sold
Variance	186 (A)

The sales volume variance is a margin variance: value it at standard profit per unit. Note that budget sales = 143 − 22 = 121 units.

Standard margin = £8 − £5 = £3 per unit.

Sales volume variance

Volume was	93 = actual number of units sold
Should have been	121 = budget number of units sold
Difference	28
At standard margin	£3 = profit per unit
Variance	£84 (A)

The price variance could be caused by a price war amongst suppliers pushing the price down, whilst the volume variance implies that the company has not competed successfully and has lost market share.

6.19 Budget profit (8,800 × £555.00 = £4,884,000)

Sales volume

Volume was	8,700
Should have been	8,800
Difference	(100)
At standard margin	£555.00
Variance	£55,500 (A)

Sales price

	£
Sales were	12,125,000
Should have been (8,700 × £1,500)	13,050,000
Variance	925,000 (A)

Material price

	£
Did pay	2,183,000
Should have paid (62,450 × £35.00)	2,185,750
Variance	2,750 (F)

Material usage

Did use	62,450 kg
Should have used (8,900 × 7)	62,300 kg
Difference	(150) kg
At standard	£35.00
Variance	£5,250 (A)

Labour rate

	£
Did pay	2,246,000
Should have paid (177,450 × £12.00)	2,129,400
Variance	116,600 (A)

Labour idle time

Idle time was	0 hour
Should have been	0 hour
Difference	0 hour
At standard	£12.00
Variance	£0

Labour efficiency

Hours were	177,450 hours
Should have been (8,900 × 20)	178,000 hours
Difference	550 hours
At standard	£12.00
Variance	£6,600 (F)

Variable overhead rate

	£
Did pay	1,435,000
Should have paid (177,450 × £8.00)	1,419,600
Variance	15,400 (A)

Variable overhead efficiency

Hours were	177,450 hours
Should have been (8,900 × 20)	178,000 hours
Difference	550 hours
At standard	£8.00
Variance	£4,400 (F)

Fixed overhead expenditure

	£
Fixed overheads were	2,650,000
Should have been (8,800 × £300.00)	2,640,000
Variance	10,000 (A)

Fixed overhead volume

Volume was	8,900 units
Should have been	8,800 units
Difference	100 units
At standard	£300.00
Variance	£30,000 (F)

Operating statement

	£
Budget profit	4,884,000
Sales volume variance	(55,500)
Flexed budget profit	4,828,500
Sales price variance	(925,000)
	3,903,500

Cost variances

	(F) £	(A) £	
Materials price	2,750		
Materials usage		5,250	
Labour rate		116,600	
Idle time			
Labour efficiency	6,600		
Variable overheads rate		15,400	
Variable overheads efficiency	4,400		
Fixed overhead expenditure		10,000	
Fixed overhead volume	30,000		
	43,750	147,250	
			(103,500)
Actual profit			£3,800,000

Proof of profit

	£	£
Sales		12,125,000
COS		
Materials used	2,183,000	
Labour	2,246,000	
Variable overheads	1,435,000	
Fixed overheads	2,650,000	
	8,514,000	
Stock (200 units × 945)	(189,000)	
COS		8,325,000
Profit		3,800,000

6.20 (a) (i) *Standard* (1 unit)

		£
Materials	1.08 units at £1.0926	1.18
Labour	1.5 min at £0.10	0.15
Variable overheads	1.5 min at £0.04	0.06
		1.39
Selling price		1.99
Profit		0.60

Budget profit (50,000 × £0.60 = £30,000)

(ii) *P&L – Actual*

	£	£
Sales		96,480
COS		
Materials used	58,450	
Labour	6,800	
Variable overheads	3,250	
	68,500	
Stock	0	
COS		68,500
Profit		27,980

(b) Variances

Sales volume

Volume was	49,700
Should have been	50,000
Difference	(300)
At standard margin	£0.60
Variance	£180 (A)

Sales price

	£
Sales were	96,480
Should have been (49,700 × £1.99)	99,903
Variance	2,423 (A)

Material price

	£
Did pay	58,450
Should have paid (55,000 × £1.0926)	60,093
Variance	1,643 (F)

Material usage

Did use	55,000 units
Should have used (49,700 × 1.08)	53,676 units
Difference	(1,324) units
At standard	£1.0926
Variance	£1,447 (A)

Labour rate

	£
Did pay	6,800
Should have paid (72,000 × £0.10)	7,200 (1,200 hours = 72,000 min)
Variance	400 (F)

Labour efficiency

Hours were	72,000 min
Should have been (49,700 × 1.5)	74,550 min
Difference	2,550 min
At standard	£0.10
Variance	£255 (F)

Variable overhead rate

	£
Did pay	3,250
Should have paid (72,000 × £0.04)	2,880
Variance	370 (A)

Variable overhead efficiency

Hours were	72,000 min
Should have been (49,700 × 1.5)	74,550 min
Difference	2,550 min
At standard	£0.04
Variance	£102 (F)

Operating statement

	£
Budget contribution	30,000
Sales volume variance	(180)
Flexed budget profit	29,820
Sales price variance	(2,423)
	27,397

Cost variances	(F)	(A)	
	£	£	
Materials price	1,643		
Materials usage		1,447	
Labour rate	400		
Labour efficiency	255		
Variable overheads rate		370	
Variable overheads efficiency	102		
	2,400	1,817	
			£583
Actual contribution			£27,980

Advanced Variance
Analysis

Advanced Variance Analysis

7

Mix and yield variances

These replace the usage variances where two or more substitutable materials are used. The price variance is unaffected.

The mix and yield variances are usually best calculated as follows, although there are alternative formats.

Mix variance

The mix variance calculates the change in costs caused by substituting one material for another.

Materials	Mix was (actual mix of actual quantity used)	Should be (standard mix of actual quantity used)	Difference	Standard price	Variance
A	x	x	x	x	x
B	x	x	x	x	x
					x

Yield variance

The yield variance calculates the change in costs caused by a change in overall usage of materials.

Yield was	x = actual output
Yield should have been	x = standard output for actual materials
Difference	x
At standard cost	x per unit of output
Variance	x

A similar set of variances can be calculated where there are two or more grades of labour in use (these are referred to as mix and productivity variances).

Sales mix and quantity variances

These occur where there are two or more products sold which are substitutes in the eyes of customers. They replace the individual volume variances.

Mix variance

Products	Mix was (actual mix of actual quantity sold)	Should be (budget mix of actual quantity sold)	Difference	Standard margin	Variance
A	x	x	x	x	x
B	x	x	x	x	x
					x

Quantity variance

Quantity was	x = actual total sales
Quantity should have been	x = budget total sales
Difference	x
At standard margin (weighted average)	x per unit of output
Variance	x

Planning and operational variances

Variances occur for many reasons (see earlier). These causes can be grouped into four categories.

Measurement factors

Errors in the capture and processing of data. For example, materials coded to the wrong account.

Planning factors

Unrealistic standards have been set. For example, unexpected inflation.

Operating factors

Day-to-day activities have deviated from plans. For example, demotivated workers.

Random factors

Also referred to as uncontrollable operating factors, these are operational issues outside of the company's control. For example, a strike at a supplier.

When a manager is faced with a large variance he should:

- ensure that the system delivers accurate, reliable information
- check the standards for reasonableness, revising them if necessary
- consider investigating any remaining variances to identify controllable factors.

✎ Exam approach

In the exam you are most likely to be tested on the revision of the standards, which splits the variance into a planning element and an operating element.

Steps

1   Read through the question identifying any planning factors (these are likely to be fairly obvious: any quantifiable reason why the standards were wrong).
2   Revise the standard cost card for these planning factors: write down a new cost card.
3   Calculate the impact of the changes you have made on the flexed budget profit – this forms the start of the operating statement:

> Original flexed budget profit   x
> Planning variance   x (balance figure)
> Revised flexed budget profit   <u>x</u>

4   Use the revised standard cost card to calculate the other variances: these are the operating variances.

5   If you need a detailed planning variance it is the difference between the original standard and the revised standard at the actual volume.

? Questions

7.1   A company has experienced a favourable mix variance on the materials that make its most popular product.

The following suggestions have been made as to the cause of this.

(i)   Extra training of employees has enabled the company to achieve lower wastage levels.
(ii)   The price of one of the component materials was reduced below standard by effective bulk-purchasing.
(iii)   The product sold higher quantities than expected at the expense of a less profitable one.

Which of these suggestions reasonably explains the variance?

A (i) only
B (ii) only
C (iii) only
D none of them

(2 marks)

7.2 A company has experienced an adverse yield variance on its raw materials.

The following suggestions have been made as to the cause of this.

  (i)   Because of a late delivery, a higher proportion of the most expensive material was used than allowed for in the standard.
  (ii) The defect rate of the finished product was higher than standard due to lower grade labour being used than normal.
  (iii) The price of one of the component materials was higher than standard due to failure to buy in bulk.

Which of these suggestions reasonably explains the variance?

A (i) only
B (ii) only
C (iii) only
D none of them

(2 marks)

7.3 A company has calculated its variances in the traditional way. Because some of its variances were exceptionally large, the company undertook further investigation and decided that the material price was understated on the standard cost card due to a planning factor.

Having extracted the planning variance the company now intends to recalculate the variances.

There is speculation that the following variances will change value.

  (i)   Material price variance
  (ii) Material usage variance
  (iii) Sales margin volume variance.

Which of these variances are most likely to change value?

A (i) and (ii) only
B (ii) and (iii) only
C (i) and (iii) only
D all of them

(2 marks)

7.4 A company operates a standard costing system. It has decided to change from absorption costing to marginal costing.

There has been some debate about which fixed overhead variances will be affected, with the following being considered.

  (i)   Fixed overhead total (cost) variance
  (ii) Fixed overhead expenditure (rate) variance
  (iii) Fixed overhead volume variance.

Which of the following represents the combination of variances that are most likely to be affected?

A   (i) and (ii) only
B   (ii) and (iii) only
C   (i) and (iii) only
D   all of them

(2 marks)

7.5   A company has decided to separately identify variances caused by planning factors.

The following causes of variances have been identified.

(i)   Inflation was significantly higher than expected, leading to adverse price variances on materials.
(ii)   A strike at a supplier led to late deliveries and no alternative had been arranged. An idle time variance was thus experienced.
(iii)   Machine maintenance was not properly scheduled leading to a high level of material wastage.

Which of the above is best described as a planning factor?

A   (i) only
B   (ii) only
C   (iii) only
D   none of them

(2 marks)

7.6   A company makes widgets, using 10 kg of material for each. After production is finished the units are checked for quality and traditionally 20% are rejected as defective.

The company has replaced some unskilled workers with skilled (but has not modified the standard cost card). As a result the defect rate of output has reduced although the amount of material going into each unit has stayed the same.

No other changes have taken place.

Which of the following is the most likely impact on the company's variances?

	Material yield	Labour mix	Labour productivity (Labour yield)
A	Favourable	Adverse	Favourable
B	None	Adverse	None
C	Favourable	None	Favourable
D	None	None	Favourable

(2 marks)

Use the following data for both the subsequent questions.
SW plc manufactures a product known as the TRD100 by mixing two materials. The standard material cost per unit of the TRD100 is as follows:

		£
Material X	12 litres at £2.50	30
Material Y	18 litres at £3.00	54

In October 2002, the actual mix used was 984 litres of X and 1,230 litres of Y. The actual output was 72 units of TRD100.

7.7 The total material mix variance reported was nearest to

A £102 (F)
B £49 (F)
C £49 (A)
D £151 (A)

(3 marks)

7.8 The total material yield variance reported was nearest to

A £102 (F)
B £49 (F)
C £49 (A)
D £151 (A)

(2 marks)

7.9 Company X makes widgets using three grades of labour, all of which are somewhat interchangeable. The company budgeted to make 320 units last month but actually produced more than this.

A standard cost card and actual cost information are shown below.

Standard (1 unit)

	Hours	£	£
Unskilled	4	5.50	22
Semi-skilled	12	6.50	78
Skilled	4	13	52
	20		152

Actual (350 units produced)

	Hours	£
Unskilled	1,440	8,150
Semi-skilled	4,330	28,150
Skilled	1,400	18,070
		54,370

Calculate the labour rate, mix and productivity (yield) variances.

(5 marks)

7.10 A pub sells four local ales. Its budget performance is below.

Budget

Ale	Pints	Price £	Revenue £	Margin £	Contribution £	(Cost) £
Old Hoppy	100	1.20	120.00	0.20	20.00	1.00
Old Peaty	200	1.40	280.00	0.22	44.00	1.18
Old Smelly	200	1.30	260.00	0.18	36.00	1.12
Old Welly	500	1.25	625.00	0.30	150.00	0.95
	1000		1,285.00		250.00	

Actual performance was slightly different.

Actual

Ale	Pints	Price £	Revenue £	Margin £	Contribution £
Old Hoppy	110	1.20	132.00	0.20	22.00
Old Peaty	220	1.36	299.20	0.18	39.60
Old Smelly	200	1.35	270.00	0.23	46.00
Old Welly	450	1.38	621.00	0.43	193.50
	980		1,322.20		301.10

Calculate the sales price, mix and quantity variances.

(5 marks)

7.11 A company budgeted to make 850 units at a standard material cost of £10,200 (4 kg per unit, £3 per kg). It achieved its target production but at a cost of £11,300 (3,120 kg).

The company had chosen to pay an extra 10% per kg to buy better quality in the hope that material usage would fall by 15%.

Treating the above as a planning factor, reconcile budget cost to actual cost, showing the planning variance.

(5 marks)

7.12 A company has a policy of investigating the cause of variances that are statistically significant. The company believes that the usage of materials per batch is normally distributed with mean of 7 kg and standard deviation of 0.2 kg.

(i) The company wishes to investigate variances that are outside of the range of 95% of outcomes, what material usage should trigger an investigation?

(3 marks)

(ii) How would your answer change if the company was only concerned about adverse variances?

(2 marks)
(Total = 5 marks)

7.13 (a) Below is a standard cost card for product X, which uses three materials.

	kg	£ per kg	£
A	7	5.00	35
B	12	6.50	78
C	6	11.00	66
	25		179

Actual production was 450 X's, the costs are detailed below.

	kg	£
A	3,200	15,500
B	5,750	38,350
C	2,150	19,575
		73,425

Requirements

Calculate the total materials variance.
Split this into price and usage variances.
Split the usage variances into mix and yield.

(10 marks)

(b)   A firm of lawyers specialises in conveyancing (registering the change of land titles). All costs are considered fixed except staff costs. Standard and budget information is below.

1 conveyance

		£
Sales price		200
Labour costs	4 hours at £20	80
Contribution		120

The budget was for 100 conveyances to be completed in the month.

Actual results were

		£
Sales	100 contracts	19,000
Labour costs	410 hours	(9,180)
Contribution		9,820

Some customers were given refunds because of mistakes made. Staff were given a 10% pay rise at the start of the month, this was not reflected in the standard cost charge.

Requirements

Reconcile budget and actual contribution identifying any planning variances.

(10 marks)
(Total = 20 marks)

7.14   T plc, a food manufacturer, has determined the following standard cost details for the three ingredients that are blended together in the processing of one of its products:

Standard cost data for 1 kg of product X

	£
0.5 kg of ingredient J at £0.50 per kg	0.25
0.3 kg of ingredient K at £1.20 per kg	0.36
0.25 kg of ingredient L at £0.80 per kg	0.20
	0.81

Actual data for March 2001 was as follows
Output of product X (000s kg) 1,650

Raw materials used

	Ingredient J	Ingredient K	Ingredient L
Quantity (000s kg)	1,072	412	396
Cost (£'000)	510	520	310

T plc does not hold any stocks of ingredients; instead, it acquires them on a JIT basis.

It is now agreed that the standard price of ingredient J was unrealistic because of a worldwide shortage. A more realistic target would have been £0.55 per kg.

Requirements

(a)   For ingredient J, calculate the planning price variance and the operating price variance.

(4 marks)

(b)   Explain why it is useful to analyse variances between planning and operating variances.

(4 marks)

(c)   Calculate the material mix variances and the material yield variance for March 2001 (on an operating basis).

(6 marks)

(d)   Comment on the meaning of the material mix variance and the yield variance.

(6 marks)
(Total = 20 marks)

✔ Answers

7.1 **D**

The materials mix variance calculates the change in costs caused by substituting one material for another. None of these suggestions refers to that.

(i)   This would be reflected in the yield variance.
(ii) This forms part of the price variance.
(iii) This is part of the sales mix variance.

7.2 **B**

An adverse yield variance means that more materials were used to produce the output than were allowed for in the standard. If the defect rate rises (for any reason) there will be a lot of material used for the actual output – an adverse yield variance.

(i)   This will produce an adverse mix variance.
(ii) This will produce a price variance.

7.3 **D**

Basically any variance where the material price is part of the calculation will change value as the material price is changed.

(i)   This will now be the difference between the *new* standard price and the actual.
(ii) This is now valued at the *new* standard price.
(iii) The margin will now be calculated as the selling price – new standard cost per unit.

7.4 **C**

    (i)   Under absorption costing this is *flexed* budget – actual, whilst under marginal costing this will be budget – actual.

    (ii)   Under both cases this will be budget – actual.

    (iii)   This does not exist under marginal costing.

7.5 **A**

Remember that a planning factor represents an error in the standard (i.e. something that should have been built into the standard if we had known about it at the time).

Only (i) fulfils this criterion – we try and build inflation into the standard at whatever level is expected.

We would not adjust the standard to allow for strikes at suppliers' nor poor machine maintenance. Note that these are problems with the company's planning function, but that does not make them "planning factors".

7.6 **A**

Material yield is favourable since there will be less material used for the actual output (after defects).

Labour mix is adverse since the skilled workers will cost more than the unskilled.

Labour productivity is favourable since the defect rate has reduced, and so less hours are needed for the actual output than originally expected.

7.7 **B**

Make sure that you have identified the fact that 30 litres of material makes one unit of output. Thus 12/30ths of the materials should be X.

Mix variance

Materials	Mix was (actual mix of actual quantity used)	Should be (standard mix of actual quantity used)	Difference	Standard price £	Variance £
X	984	885.6*	(98.4)	2.50	(246)
Y	1,230	1,328.4**	98.4	3.00	295
	2,214	2,214	0		49 (F)

* 12/30 × 2,214 = 885.6

** 18/30 × 2,214 = 1,328.4

7.8 **D**

Yield variance

Yield was	72	= actual output
Yield should have been (2,214 ÷ 30)	73.8	= standard output for actual materials
Difference	1.8	
At standard cost (£30 + £54)	£84	= per unit of output
Variance	£151	(A)

7.9 Although it feels different, mix and productivity variances for labour are calculated the same way as mix and yield for materials.

Rate variance

	Did pay	Should pay	Difference
Unskilled	8,150	7,920	(230)
Semi-skilled	28,150	28,145	(5)
Skilled	18,070	18,200	130
Total			£105 (A)

Mix variance

	Mix was	Should be	Difference	Standard rate	Variance
Unskilled	1,440	1,434	(6)	5.50	(33)
Semi-skilled	4,330	4,302	(28)	6.50	(182)
Skilled	1,400	1,434	34	13	442
	7,170		0		£227 (F)

Productivity variance

Yield was	350
Should be (7,170 ÷ 20)	358.5
Difference	(8.5)
Standard	152
Variance	£1,292 (A)

7.10 *Price variance* (remember this is a revenue variance).

Ale	Revenue was £	(Actual) Pints	(Standard) Price £	Should have been £	Variance £
Old Hoppy	132.00	110	1.20	132.00	0.00 (F)
Old Peaty	299.20	220	1.40	308.00	(8.80) (A)
Old Smelly	270.00	200	1.30	260.00	10.00 (F)
Old Welly	621.00	450	1.25	562.50	58.50 (F)
	1,322.20			1,262.50	59.70 (F)

Mix variance (remember this is a margin variance).

Ale	Mix was	Should be (%)	Should be (units)	Difference	Standard margin £	Variance £
Old Hoppy	110	10	98	12	0.20	2.40 (F)
Old Peaty	220	20	196	24	0.22	5.28 (F)
Old Smelly	200	20	196	4	0.18	0.72 (F)
Old Welly	450	50	490	(40)	0.30	12.00 (A)
	980		980	0		3.60 (A)

Quantity variance (remember this is a margin variance).

Quantity was	980 pints
Should have been	1000 pints
Difference	(20) pints
Standard margin (£250 ÷ 1000 pints)	£0.25
	£5 (A)

7.11 Always calculate the original standard cost and the revised standard cost before calculating planning variances.

Original standard cost: 4.0 kg × £3.00 per kg = £12.00

Revised standard cost: 3.4 kg × £3.30 per kg = £11.22

	£	£
Original budget cost (£12.00 × 850)		10,200
Planning variance (to balance)		(663) (F)
Revised budget cost (£11.22 × 850)		9,537
Operating variances		
Did pay	11,300	
Should have paid (3,120 × £3.30)	10,296	
Variance		1,004 (A)
Did use	3,120 kg	
Should have used (850 × 3.4 kg)	2,890 kg	
Difference	230 kg	
At standard price	£3.30	
Variance		759 (A)
		11,300

Note that an adverse variance represents an increase to costs, so it must be added to the total.

7.12 (i) From tables: 95% of outcomes occur within 1.96 standard deviations of the mean (look up 0.475 in the body of the table).

Thus, variances should be investigated if they are more than 1.96 standard deviations from the mean.

Investigate a variance if, either

the average usage is above $7 + 1.96 \times 0.2 = 7.392$ kg, or

the average usage is below $7 - 1.96 \times 0.2 = 6.608$ kg

(ii) From tables: 95% of outcomes occur below 1.645 standard deviations of the mean (look up 0.45 in the body of the table).

Thus, variances should be investigated if they are more than 1.645 standard deviations above the mean.

Investigate a variance if the average usage is above $7 + 1.645 \times 0.2 = 7.329$ kg

7.13   (a)   Total materials variance

Actual   *Flexed budget*   *Total variance*

£73,425   £179 × 450 units = £80,550   £7,125 (F)

Price variance

	Did pay	Should pay	Difference
A	£15,500	3,200 kg × £5.00 = £16,000	£500
B	£38,350	5,750 kg × £6.50 = £37,375	£(975)
C	£19,575	2,150 kg × £11.00 = £23,650	£4,075
Total			£3,600 (F)

Usage variances

	Did use (kg)	Should use (kg)	Difference (kg)	Standard price (£)	Variance (£)
A	3,200	3,150	(50)	5.00	(250)
B	5,750	5,400	(350)	6.50	(2,275)
C	2,150	2,700	550	11.00	6,050
Total					3,525 (F)

Note: Price + Usage = Total

Mix variance

	Mix was (kg)	Should be (kg)	Difference	Standard price (£)	Variance (£)
A	3,200	7/25 × 11,100 = 3,108	(92.0)	5.00	(460)
B	5,750	12/25 × 11,100 = 5,328	(422.0)	6.50	(2,743)
C	2,150	6/25 × 11,100 = 2,664	514.0	11.00	5,654
Total	11,100		0.0		2,451 (F)

Yield variance

Yield was	450 units
Should be	11,100/25 = 444 units
Difference	6 units
Standard	£179
Variance	£1,074 (F)

Note: Mix + Yield = Usage

(b)   Revise the standard cost card for the wage rise – it is the only planning factor.

1 contract

		£
Sales price		200
Labour costs	4 hours at £22	88
Contribution		112

Operating statement

	£	£
Original budget contribution (£120 × 100 contracts)	12,000	
Planning variance (to balance):		800 (A)
Revised budget contribution (£112 × 100 contracts)		11,200
Sales price variance:		
Revenue was	19,000	
Should have been (100 × £200)	20,000	
Variance		£1,000 (A)
Labour rate variance:		
Did pay	9,180	
Should pay (410 hours × £22)	9,020	
Variance		£160 (A)
Labour efficiency variance:		
Hours were	410	
Should be (100 × 4 hours)	400	
	10	
Standard rate (revised)	22	
Variance		£220 (A)
Actual contribution		£9,820

7.14 (a) *Planning price variance*

	£
Revised standard cost (1,650 × 0.5 kg × £0.55)	453.75
Original standard cost (1,650 × 0.5 kg × £0.50)	412.50
	41.25 (A)

Operating price variance

	£
1,072 kg did cost	510.00
But should have cost (1,072 × £0.55)	589.60
	79.60 (F)

(b) Variances should be analysed between planning and operating causes, so that management can focus on controllable costs and revenues. A planning variance represents the difference between an original standard, which is no longer considered to be a relevant or achievable target, and a revised standard. Such variances, therefore, represent uncontrollable differences between the actual and target performance. Operating variances arise by comparing actual performance against achievable targets. Such variances are thus considered to be controllable by management decisions and actions.

(c) *Material mix variances*

Revised average standard price/kg of input:

	£
0.5 kg of J at £0.55/kg	0.275
0.3 kg of K at £1.20/kg	0.360
0.25 kg of L at £0.80/kg	0.200
	0.835

$$\frac{£0.835}{1.05 \text{ kg}} = £0.795/\text{kg of input}$$

Mix variance

Materials	Mix was (actual mix of actual quantity used)	Should be (standard mix of actual quantity used)	Difference	Standard price £	Variance £
J	1,072	895	(177)	0.55	(97.35)
K	412	537	125	1.20	150.00
L	396	448	52	0.80	41.60
	1,880	1,880	0		94.25 (F)

Yield variance

	kg
1,880 kg input should yield (1,880/1.05)	1,790.48
Actual yield	1,650.00
	140.48

140.48 kg shortfall at £0.835 = £117.30 (A).

(d) The material mix variance shows the reduction in costs caused by the substitution of cheaper materials for more expensive. In this case more of J (least expensive) and less of K and L.

It is not clear that this actually represents an improvement for the company. A short-term saving in costs may lead to a reduction in product quality with consequent repair costs.

The standard was set at, presumably, an appropriate mix. A deviation from this may represent a reduction in customer satisfaction (consider increasing the cheaper materials in a cake mix) with subsequent losses of sales in the future.

The adverse yield variance represents a reduction in output compared with standard.

This may be connected with the mix variance: a change in mix may lead to greater defective output. If this is the case then, on balance, the change in mix was not beneficial.

The yield variance may not be connected with the mix variance; it could be due to poor quality labour (unskilled or demotivated) or machine breakdowns, leading to defective output.

Budgeting

Budgeting

8

> 🔑 A budget is a quantified plan of future activities.

Purpose of budgeting

Benefits

Use the mnemonic "crumpet" to help remember the main benefits of budgeting.

- Co-ordination (of activities)
- Responsibility (clearly allocated)
- Utilisation (of resources)
- Motivation
- Planning
- Evaluation (of performance)
- Telling (communication).

Traditional budgets

Fixed budgets

A fixed budget is prepared under a given set of assumptions.

Steps

- Identify the principal budget factor
- Produce the budget for the principal budget factor
- Produce the production budget
- Other budgets.

Limiting factor analysis may be needed if the principal budget factor is anything other than sales.

Flexible budgets

These are budgets which are valid under different sets of assumptions.
In some cases this leads to several budgets being prepared.

Many organisations budget flexibly with the use of computers, spreadsheets being the simplest approach used.

Flexed budgets

A flexed budget is used to assess performance.

The original budget is adjusted (flexed) to take account of changes in activity levels.

Recent developments in budgeting

Systems approach

An organisation is a social system. Like other systems it has inputs, a process and outputs.

Budgetary control is a form of feedback control in that it tries to identify (and thus correct) deviations from plan; it can be

- positive, to reinforce a beneficial deviation
- negative, to reduce a detrimental deviation.

Budgetary control is also a form of feedforward control in that it tries to anticipate deviations from planned performance.

Zero-based budgeting

It is an attempt to replace the use of incremental budgets in service environments. It uses decision-packages to identify activities that can be undertaken by a department, together with their costs.

Steps

- Identify possible activities that a department can undertake
- Estimate the costs necessary for each activity
- Combine these into decision-packages
- Undertake cost–benefit analysis on the packages
- Rank packages
- Allocate funds between departments until total funds are utilised or the cost exceeds the benefit.

Activity-based budgeting (ABB)

Budgeting is based around activities rather than physical locations. It uses similar principles to activity-based costing.

Rolling budgets

Budgets are prepared on an ongoing basis, adding one month's budget to the end of a period as the current month passes.

These represent an attempt to replace the annual budgeting round with a system that spreads the workload more evenly and is inherently more up to date.

? Questions

8.1 Company X makes widgets. The following information relates to the year just passed.

Standard cost of one widget = £38
Actual cost of one widget = £39

Budget output = 5,150 widgets
Budget sales = 4,800 widgets
Actual output = 5,100 widgets
Actual stock increase = 250 widgets.

There were no opening stocks.

What is the flexed budget cost of production?

A   £184,300
B   £193,800
C   £195,700
D   £198,900

(2 marks)

8.2 The widget company has been operating a standard costing system for some years. The following information relates to a recent year.

Budget output = 28,200 widgets
Budget stock increase = 1,200 widgets

Actual stock increase = 1,300 widgets
Actual sales = 28,900 widgets

Standard cost of one widget = £17
Actual cost of one widget = £15.

There were no opening stocks.

What is the flexed budget cost of production?

A   £453,000
B   £479,400
C   £491,300
D   £513,400

(2 marks)

8.3 In a manufacturing company each worker can produce four units per hour.

After units are produced they are inspected and 10% are typically found to be defective. Workers spend four hours each per week on non-productive tasks.

The normal working week is 37 hours paid at £7.00/hour.
There are 25 workers.
Budget sales are 3,150 per week.

Any overtime is paid at time and a half.
The company holds no stocks.

Which of the following is closest to the weekly labour cost budget?

A £6,475
B £6,825
C £6,910
D £7,000

(3 marks)

8.4 A factory shuts down for two weeks every year for production staff holiday and maintenance purposes. This year it is closing for Weeks 32 and 33. Functions other than production continue to operate.

In order that customers are continually supplied, the company builds up its completed stock prior to the shut down. Normally stocks are kept at one week.

Demand is regular at 18,000 units per month. Production capacity is 32,000 units per month.

Materials are 0.04 kg per unit. Material stocks equal to the next two weeks' production requirements are held.

Assuming that the stock policy is adhered to all year, which of the following is the closest to the material purchases for Week 29?

A 720 kg
B 1,040 kg
C 1,240 kg
D 1,280 kg

(4 marks)

8.5 A company is expecting demand for its product to grow significantly, but is trying to constrain its growth in stocks.

Sales in January: 2,500 units
Stocks, 1st January: 500 units

Growth rate of sales: 25% per month.
Stock policy: to grow at 15% per month.

Which of the following is closest to the budgeted production in March?

A 3,210 units
B 3,810 units
C 4,010 units
D 4,880 units

(2 marks)

8.6 A company makes product Z. Target sales are 18,900 units.

After production the units are quality checked and 10% of all units produced are found to be defective. These have to be scrapped.

Each unit produced requires 25 kg of material.

The company has opening stocks of 1,500 units of Z and wishes closing stocks to be 2,400 units. Units are not transferred to stock until after quality checking. Raw material stocks are 30,000 kg and are budgeted to fall by 10%.

Which of the following is the nearest to budgeted purchases of material?

A   526,750 kg
B   544,500 kg
C   547,000 kg
D   553,000 kg

(3 marks)

8.7   A company's costs for January were budgeted at £16,300. For February they were budgeted at £14,300.

Budgeted output for January was 4,800 units and for February 4,200 units.

Any output level over 4,500 units requires an extra £200 spending on maintenance of the equipment.

Budgeted output for March was 4,600 units whilst actual output was 4,700 units.

Which of the following is the nearest to the flexed budget cost for March?

A   £15,700
B   £15,800
C   £16,000
D   £17,400

(3 marks)

8.8   The following statements relate to companies that flex their budgets in order to assess performance.

(i)   For a company using absorption costing, the fixed overheads are flexed to take account of the difference between budget and actual production levels.
(ii)   For a company using marginal costing, the costs may be flexed on different bases to reflect the different factors that affect the costs.

	Statement (i)	Statement (ii)
A	True	True
B	True	False
C	False	True
D	False	False

(2 marks)

8.9   The following comments relate to zero-based budgeting (ZBB).

(i)   Zero-based budgeting often replaces incremental budgeting which tends to encourage employees to submit excessive budgets.
(ii)   Zero-based budgeting creates a complete cost budget by summing relevant costs contained in decision-packages.
(iii)   Zero-based budgeting is an attempt to ensure that service departments and companies can justify the costs budgeted for.

Which of these statements are substantially true?

A   (i) and (ii) only
B   (ii) and (iii) only
C   (i) and (iii) only
D   all of them

(2 marks)

8.10   The following statements concern incremental budgeting.

(i)   The production of incremental budgets is easier, quicker and requires less-skilled staff than zero-based budgeting.

(ii)   Incremental budgeting concentrates on highlighting the increase in variable costs arising as a result of corporate growth.

(iii)   Incremental budgeting starts with past figures and adjusts for anticipated changes, whether environmental or internal.

Which of these statements are substantially true?

A   (i) and (ii) only
B   (ii) and (iii) only
C   (i) and (iii) only
D   all of them

(2 marks)

8.11   The following statements concern rolling budgets.

(i)   Rolling budgets are more able to deal with environmental uncertainty than traditional budgeting methods.

(ii)   Rolling budgets lead to a more evenly spread workload for the planners than traditional budgets.

(iii)   Rolling budgets produce more consistency as regards planning horizons than traditional budgeting techniques.

Which of these statements are substantially true?

A   (i) and (ii) only
B   (ii) and (iii) only
C   (i) and (iii) only
D   all of them

(2 marks)

8.12   A company makes a product which is very seasonal in demand, peaking in March. The company's production capacity is 1,400 units per month and therefore it produces sufficient units at the start of the year to keep supplying customers in March from stock.

Each unit requires 3 kg of material.

Demand for the product is as follows:

	Jan	Feb	Mar	Apr
Demand	800	1,200	2,700	400

From the end of January, the company's policy will be to have sufficient stock of material for half of the next month's production requirements. The finished good stock will be nil except where it is necessary to hold stocks prior to the seasonal peak.

Stocks are currently (beginning of January) 750 completed units and 3,000 kg of material.

What is the required purchase of materials in January?

(5 marks)

8.13 What is a rolling budget and when may it be more appropriate than traditional budgeting techniques?

(5 marks)

8.14 What is feedback and feedforward control? Give an example of each from a budgeting perspective.

(5 marks)

8.15 Explain the concepts of positive and negative feedback. Give an example of each from a budgeting perspective.

(5 marks)

8.16 What are the main advantages of a zero-based budgeting system?

(5 marks)

8.17 State why organisations prepare budgets.

(5 marks)

8.18 For a number of years, the research division of Z plc has produced its annual budget (for new and continuing projects) using incremental budgeting techniques. The company is now under new management and the annual budget for 2004 is to be prepared using zero-based budgeting techniques.

Requirements

(a) Explain the differences between incremental and zero-based budgeting techniques.

(5 marks)

(b) Explain how Z plc could operate a zero-based budgeting system for its research projects.

(8 marks)

The operating divisions of Z plc have in the past always used a traditional approach to analysing costs into their fixed and variable components. A single measure of activity was used, which, for simplicity, was the number of units produced. The new management does not accept that such a simplistic approach is appropriate for budgeting in the modern environment and has requested that the managers adopt an activity-based approach to their budgets for 2004.

Requirements

(c) (i) Briefly explain ABB.

(3 marks)

(ii) Briefly explain how ABB would be implemented by the operating divisions of Z plc.

(4 marks)
(Total = 20 marks)

8.19 Two products are manufactured by a company in one of its factories. The products comprise different mixes of two basic materials. One grade of direct labour is employed in the mixing process and another grade in final packaging.

Current (pre-2006) standard direct material and direct labour costs for the two products in the current period are

Product	Y	Z
	(£ per 100 units)	(£ per 100 units)
material A	156	78
material B	54	72
mixing labour	11.25	11.25
packaging labour	20.00	20.00

The current (pre-2006) standard prices/rates are

material A	£5.20 per kg
material B	£1.80 per kg
mixing labour	£4.50 per hour
packaging labour	£4.00 per hour

The company is now engaged in preparing its 2006 budget.

A favourable usage variance has been consistently achieved in the past on material A. It has been decided to incorporate this variance into the standard. In the past, 12.5% of material A losses (losses/productive input) were incorporated into the standard but in 2006 this standard loss was revised to 10%.

Standard material prices are to be lifted by 5% and standard labour rates by 8% in 2006.

The sales budget for 2006 has been determined as follows:

Product Y	1.7 million units
Product Z	0.95 million units

Existing and budget inventory levels are as follows:

	End 2005	End 2006
material A	40,000 kg	25,000 kg
material B	95,000 kg	90,000 kg
Product Y	190,000 units	200,000 units
Product Z	150,000 units	125,000 units

Requirements

(a) Calculate the standard material and labour costs for both products in 2006, showing your workings in full detail.

(8 marks)

(b) Calculate (i) the budget production (in units) for both products in 2006 (ii) the procurement budget (in kg) for materials A and B in 2006 and (iii) the mixing and packaging labour hour requirement budget (in hours) for 2006. Show your full workings in all cases.

(9 marks)

(c) Prepare a labour and material production cost budget for the whole operation in 2006 with inventories (materials and finished goods) all valued on the FIFO principle.

(8 marks)

(Total = 25 marks)

☑ **Answers**

8.1 **B**

Do not forget that flexed budget is the *standard cost of actual output* = 5,100 × £38 = £193,800.

8.2 **D**

Do not forget that flexed budget is the *standard cost of actual output* = (28,900 + 1,300) × £17 = £513,400.

8.3 **D**

Note that sales can only represent 90% of output, so we must multiply sales by 100/90 to get production.

Required good production = 3,150

Total production (3,150 × 100/90)	3,500 units
Total productive hours required (3,500 ÷ 4)	875 hours
Non-productive time (25 × 4)	100 hours
Total hours	975 hours
Normal hours available (25 × 37)	925 hours
Required overtime	50 hours
Normal cost (925 hours × £7)	£6,475
Overtime (50 hours × £7 × 150%)	£525
Total	£7,000

8.4 **D**

The company presumably already has 18,000 units of completed stock, and it wishes this to remain in place all year. You therefore only need to deal with any stock levels above this.

At the start of the shutdown (end W31), there must be sufficient extra stock of completed units for all W32 and W33. That is, 2 × 18,000 units = 36,000 units.

The company only has spare capacity of 32,000 − 18,000 = 14,000 units/week. Therefore the build-up of stock will take in excess of two weeks.

	Units
Total excess production required	36,000
Total excess production W31	(14,000)
Total excess production W30	(14,000)
Total excess production W29	8,000

	W28	*W29*	*W30*	*W31*
Production	18,000	26,000	32,000	32,000
Usage (kg)	720	1,040	1,280	1,280
Opening stock in kg (2W)	(1,760)	(2,320)	(2,560)	(1,280)
Closing stock (kg)	2,320	2,560	1,280	0
Purchases (kg)	1,280	1,280	40	0

8.5 **C**

Since the growth rate of stock is slower than sales we need to do a full budget.

	Jan	Feb	Mar
Sales	2,500	3,125	3,906
Opening stock	(500)	(575)	(661)
Closing stock	575	661	760
Production	2,575	3,211	4,005

8.6 **C**

Note that sales can only represent 90% of output, so we must multiply sales by 100/90 to get production.

Make sure that you adjust for the stock correctly.

Target sales	18,900 units
Stock increase (2,400 − 1,500)	900 units
Required good output	19,800 units
Total output required (19,800 × 100/90)	22,000 units
Materials required (25 kg × 22,000)	550,000 kg
Less stock reduction	3,000 kg
Required purchases	547,000 kg

8.7 **C**

We need to use the high–low method to split costs into fixed and variable.

Deal with the maintenance spending separately.

Remember that flexed budget is the budgeted cost adjusted to actual output.

	Output (units)	Cost (£)
Jan (excluding maintenance)	4,800	16,100
Feb	4,200	14,300
	600	1,800

	£
Variable cost/unit (£1,800 ÷ 600)	3
Fixed costs (excluding maintenance)	
(£14,300 − £3 × 4,200)	1,700
Flexed budget for March (including maintenance)	
(£1,700 + £3 × 4,700 + £200)	16,000

8.8 **A**

(i) This is only true for absorption costing systems.

(ii) This is true for marginal and absorption costing systems, for example, production costs are flexed according to production levels, whilst sales costs are flexed according to sales levels.

8.9 **D**

Zero-based budgeting uses decision-packages to consider the costs and benefits that relate to service based situations. Costs should thus be justified.

The traditional approach in these situations is to base the budget on the past with increments for inflation and growth. This encourages employees to "pad" their budget submissions.

Thus all points are true.

8.10 **C**

Incremental budgeting applies to service areas and involves taking last year's figures (or similar) and adjusting for factors such as growth, changes in policy and inflation.

(i) Incremental budgeting is relatively straightforward.
(ii) Variable costs are relatively rare in situations where incremental budgeting is used.
(iii) This is what it does.

8.11 **D**

A rolling budget with a three-month horizon would start a year with the budget for January, February and March already prepared. During January the April budget would be prepared, during February the May budget would be prepared, etc.

This means that

(i) budgets are prepared fairly close to when they are needed, leading to less need to predict an uncertain environment
(ii) the workload is spread over the whole year
(iii) the planning horizon is fixed (at three months in the example) rather than starting at 12+ months at the start of the year, and reducing as the year progresses.

8.12 You will need to work backwards to calculate required production in January and then calculate purchases. Remember to adjust for stock.

Sales in March	2,700
Production in March (max)	(1,400)
Required stock at end of February	1,300
Sales in February	1,200
Production in February	(1,400)
Required stock at end of January	1,100
Sales in January	800
Opening stock in January	(750)
Required production in January	1,150
Purchases for January production (3 kg × 1,150)	3,450 kg
Closing stock (3 kg × 1,400 × 0.5)	2,100 kg
Less opening stock	(3,000) kg
Purchases	2,550 kg

8.13 A rolling budget is a budget prepared with a fixed planning horizon. To achieve this, the budget is constantly being added to at the same rate as time is passing.

For example, a company with a three-month rolling budget would start a new year with January–March's budget done. Then during January the April budget would be prepared, during February the May budget would be prepared, etc.

Rolling budgets can be very useful for companies experiencing rapid change, as they require forecasting for much shorter time periods.

Rolling budgets can also be useful for very seasonal businesses, especially where the peak of work is towards the year end as they spread the work out more evenly.

Rolling budgets are useful in dynamic environments where the nature of change is unpredictable. In these situations whole (12 month) budgets can be rendered obsolete by environmental change.

8.14 A feedback control involves obtaining information on actual results from the process and comparing with control data (a plan). Deviations from the control data will usually prompt control action in order to bring actual results back in line with plan.

Feedforward control works on the basis of forecast results; it is therefore anticipating problems and then dealing with them.

Traditional variance analysis is an example of a feedback control: actual costs are compared with a (flexed) budget and control action is taken.

Feedforward control usually takes place at the planning stage: if the cash budget forecasts that the overdraft limit is likely to be breached then remedial action is taken.

8.15 A feedback control involves obtaining information on actual results from the process and comparing with control data (a plan).

When the deviation from plan is considered undesirable then the control action is designed to reduce it. This is termed negative feedback.

When the deviation from plan is considered desirable then the control action is designed to increase it. This is termed positive feedback.

Generally an adverse variance will produce negative feedback: an adverse material price variance may reinforce the policy of bulk buying to obtain discounts.

Some favourable variances lead to positive feedback. For example, a customer care course might lead to sales exceeding budget in a branch: management would certainly consider extending this to other parts of the business.

8.16 A zero-based budgeting system involves splitting activities and their associated costs into decision-packages and then ranking them before allocating resources.

Zero-based budgeting has the following advantages claimed for it.

It avoids the complacency inherent in the traditional incremental approach, where it is assumed that future activities will be very similar to current ones.

Zero-based budgeting encourages a questioning approach, by focusing attention not only on the cost of an activity, but also on the benefits it provides.

Preparation of the decision-packages will normally require the involvement of many employees, and thus provides an opportunity for their view to be considered. This involvement may produce useful ideas, and promote job satisfaction among the wider staff.

Zero-based budgeting should help to reduce budget padding in that excessive budgets will be rejected since their benefits will not cover their costs.

8.17   There are a number of reasons why organisations prepare budgets. These include

- the formalisation of plans
- the motivation of managers
- the basis of comparison with actual performance
- the need to coordinate activities
- the anticipation of problems.

8.18   (a)   The main differences between incremental and zero-based budgeting may be summarised as follows:

Incremental budgets are budgets that are based on past budget or actual results, adjusted for expected volume and price level changes. As a result, they assume that previous activities continue to be appropriate and that previous efficiency levels are reasonable targets.

Zero-based budgets require each activity to be justified by the manager responsible. Once the activity has been justified, its method of operation and related cost need to be justified on a cost/benefit basis. This requires a detailed consideration of the business and how it operates, and thus is much more time-consuming and therefore costlier than incremental budgeting.

(b)   Z plc could operate a zero-based budgeting system for its projects by considering each of its projects individually. For each research project that has been started before the introduction of the zero-based budgeting system, there would need to be an evaluation that considered its future costs and future benefits. If a project's predicted benefits do not exceed expected future costs, it should be abandoned.

For new projects, a cost–benefit analysis needs to be carried out that looks carefully at each proposed new project. For each new project, the alternative research methods must be considered in terms of the activities involved and the support systems required. The costs and benefits of these alternatives must then be evaluated, and the project ranked according to its value to Z plc.

The ranking of all of the projects would then be considered by the senior managers of Z plc. They consider the costs and potential benefits to the company as a whole, and select which projects are to be undertaken using the funds that have been made available to the research division.

(c)   (i)   Activity-based budgeting is the technique of budgeting that focuses on the outputs of an organisation rather than the more traditional approach of budgeting from an input perspective.

This form of budgeting requires that managers identify the activities that cause costs to be incurred rather than relying on a single output measure and assuming that all costs are either affected by it (variable costs) or not affected by it (fixed costs).

(ii)   To implement ABB, the managers of the operating divisions of Z plc will need to consider the activities involved in each of the products and services that they provide, and then consider how the carrying out of these activities causes costs to be incurred.

The managers would then need to relate their output targets to the activities required to complete them and then determine the cost of carrying out these activities.

The final budget would show the cost budgeted for each activity rather than the traditional cost headings of (for example) materials and labour.

8.19 (a)

2005 standards, per 100 units

Product Y	kg/hrs	rate £	std £
mat A	30	5.20	156.00
mat B	30	1.80	54.00
mix lab	2.5	4.50	11.25
pack lab	5	4.00	20.00
total			241.25

Product Z	kg/hrs	rate £	std £
mat A	15	5.20	78.00
mat B	40	1.80	72.00
mix lab	2.5	4.50	11.25
pack lab	5	4.00	20.00
total			181.25

2006 standards, per 100 units

Product Y	kg/hrs	rate £	std £
mat A	29.33	5.46	160.16
mat B	30	1.89	56.70
mix lab	2.5	4.86	12.15
pack lab	5	4.32	21.60
total			250.61

Note: A kg = 30/1.125 × 1.1

Product Z	kg/hrs	rate £	std £
mat A	14.67	5.46	80.08
mat B	40	1.89	75.60
mix lab	2.5	4.86	12.15
pack lab	5	4.32	21.60
total			189.43

(b)

   (i)   Production units

	Y	Z
sales	1,700,000	950,000
op stock	190,000	150,000
cl stock	200,000	125,000
production	1,710,000	9,25,000

   (ii) Material Procurement kg

	A	B
usage	637,267	883,000
op stock	40,000	95,000
cl stock	25,000	90,000
procured	622,267	878,000

   (iii) Labour usage hours

	Mix	Pack
Y	42,750	85,500
Z	23,125	46,250
total	65,875	131,750

(c)

Opening Stock:
material A	208,000
material B	171,000
product Y	458,375
product Z	271,875
total	1,109,250

Procurement and Wages
material A	3,397,576
material B	1,659,420
mix lab	320,153
pack lab	569,160
total	5,946,309

Closing Stock:
material A	136,500
material B	170,100
product Y	501,220
product Z	236,788
total	1,044,608

Production Costs: 6,010,951

Budgeting
for Performance
and People

Budgeting for Performance and People

9

Behavioural issues

Budgets are an attempt to direct staff. If they are not properly prepared they will demotivate staff.

In order to avoid this, the following should be true

- Targets should be hard but achievable
- Rewards and incentives should be used to recognise good performance
- Staff should be allowed to participate in the budget-setting process
- Targets should be properly communicated to staff
- Staff alone should be held accountable for aspects of performance that they control
- Budgets should be goal congruent
- Budgets should cover more than just financial performance.

Budgets need to be flexed to actual activity level in order to properly assess performance; this is part of the control concept discussed above.

A budgetary control statement compares flexed budget with actual performance for each cost heading. This produces total variance figures.

Top down vs bottom up

Top-down budgets are prepared by senior managers and planners, and imposed on staff.

Bottom-up budgets are set by more junior staff and aggregated to form total budgets.

Advantages of top down are

- it is faster
- it is goal congruent
- budgets are well coordinated
- no excessive slack is built in.

Disadvantages of top down are

- it can demotivate staff
- less input from those with practical experience
- requires central planning staff
- less flexibility.

In practice neither system is as extreme as implied by these terms: top-down budgets are often modified based on feedback from staff, and bottom up are sent back to staff where they are too slack or unrealistic.

Performance targets for budgets

Profitability

The main aim of a company, this links well to corporate goals.

Targets can be net profit margin, gross profit margin, return on investment and residual income.

There may be conflict between the long and short term.

Liquidity

Usually viewed as an indicator of corporate survival.

Targets can be current ratio, quick ratio or individual working capital ratios such as debtors days.

Asset turnover

An indicator of asset efficiency or corporate strategy.

Note: return on investment = asset turnover $\times$ net profit margin.

? Questions

9.1 The following statements relate to whether a top-down or bottom-up budgeting system is used by a company.

(i) Bottom-up budgeting leads to increased goal congruence between the parts of the organisation.

(ii) Top-down budgeting is often criticised for leading to demotivated staff who feel remote from the organisation.

(iii) Top-down budgeting tends to be a faster process to apply than bottom-up budgeting.

Which of these statements are substantially true?

A   (i) and (ii) only
B   (ii) and (iii) only
C   (i) and (iii) only
D   all of them

(2 marks)

9.2   A service company evaluates its performance using a number of key ratios. This includes the current ratio which is targeted not to fall below a value of 2.

Forecasts to date predict that debtors will fluctuate between £135,000 and £142,000, and creditors between £17,000 and £22,000. The company has no stocks.

Which of the following represents the closest to the maximum budgeted overdraft permitted if the company is to achieve its target?

A   £45,500
B   £49,800
C   £54,000
D   £248,000

(2 marks)

9.3   A division has a return on investment of 18% and an asset turnover of two times.

Which of the following is closest to the division's net profit margin?

A   9%
B   16%
C   20%
D   36%

(2 marks)

9.4   The purpose of a flexible budget is

A   to cap discretionary expenditure.
B   to produce a revised forecast by changing the original budget when actual costs are known.
C   to control resource efficiency.
D   to communicate target activity levels within an organisation by setting a budget in advance of the period to which it relates.

(2 marks)

9.5   A company evaluates its performance using a number of key ratios. This includes the current ratio which is targeted not to fall below a value of 1.7.

Forecasts for the elements of working capital are stocks £14,800, debtors £19,600 and creditors £144,000.

Which of the following represents the closest to the minimum budgeted bank balance permitted if the company is to achieve its target?

A   £50,306
B   £109,600
C   £210,400
D   £279,200

(2 marks)

9.6 A division has a net profit margin of 16% and an asset turnover of 0.9 times.

Which of the following is closest to the division's return on investment?

A 14.4%
B 15.1%
C 16.9%
D 17.8%

(2 marks)

9.7 In the context of budget preparation, the term "goal congruence" is

A the alignment of budgets with objectives using feedforward control.
B the setting of a budget which does not include budget bias.
C the alignment of corporate objectives with the personal objectives of a manager.
D the use of aspiration levels to set efficiency targets.

(2 marks)

9.8 Which of the following statements is/are true?

(i) A flexible budget can be used to control operational efficiency.
(ii) Incremental budgeting is a system of budgetary planning and control that measures the additional costs of the extra units of activity.
(iii) Participative budgeting is a method of centralised budgeting that uses a top-down approach and aspiration levels.

A (i) and (ii) only
B (ii) and (iii) only
C (iii) only
D (i) only

(2 marks)

9.9 Budgets can act as an incentive to managers to act in ways that are not congruent with organisational goals. Give some examples of this.

(5 marks)

9.10 What are the qualities of a good budgetary control report?

(5 marks)

9.11 What are the qualities of a good monthly management-accounting report?

(5 marks)

9.12 What are the main benefits of including managers in the budget-setting process?

(5 marks)

9.13 R plc is an engineering company that repairs machinery and manufactures replacement parts for machinery used in the building industry. There are a number of different departments in the company including a foundry, a grinding department, a milling department and a general machining department. R plc prepared its budget for the year ending 31 December 2003 using an incremental budgeting system.

The budget is set centrally and is then communicated to each of the managers who has responsibility for achieving their respective targets. The following report has been produced for the general machining department for October 2003:

	Budget	Actual	Variance
Number of machine hours	9,000	11,320	2,320 (F)
	$	$	$
Cleaning materials	1,350	1,740	390 (A)
Steel	45,000	56,000	11,000 (A)
Other direct materials	450	700	250 (A)
Direct labour	29,000	32,400	3,400 (A)
Production overheads	30,000	42,600	12,600 (A)
Total	105,800	133,440	27,640 (A)

The Manager of the general machining department has received a memo from the Financial Controller, requiring him to explain the serious overspending within his department.

The Manager has sought your help and, after some discussion, you have ascertained the following:

- the cleaning materials, steel and other direct materials vary in proportion to the number of machine hours
- the budgeted direct labour costs include fixed salary costs of $4,250, the balance is variable in proportion to the number of machine hours
- the production overhead costs include a variable cost that is constant per machine hour at all activity levels, and a stepped fixed cost which changes when the activity level exceeds 10,000 machine hours. A further analysis of this cost is shown below:

Activity (machine hours)	3,000	7,000	14,000
Costs ($)	13,500	24,500	45,800

Requirements

(a) Prepare a revised budgetary control statement using the additional information that you have obtained from the Manager of the general machining department. Comment on your findings.

(12 marks)

(b) (i) Explain the differences between an incremental budgeting system and a zero-based budgeting system.

(4 marks)

(ii) Explain why R plc and similar organisations would find it difficult to introduce a system of zero-based budgeting.

(4 marks)
(Total = 20 marks)

✓ **Answers**

9.1 **B**

(i) One of the problems of bottom-up budgeting is that each part of the organisation tends to pursue its own goals.
(ii) This is due to the budget being imposed on staff.
(iii) Bottom-up budgets are usually compared with overall company targets and then revised.

9.2 **A**

The ratio is at its lowest when debtors are low and creditors high.

Thus the debtors (£135,000) must be double the combined overdraft and creditors (i.e. £67,500).

O/d = £67,500 − £22,000 = £45,500.

Or using algebra:

135,000 = 2(22,000 + o/d)
 67,500 = 22,000 + o/d
    o/d = 45,500.

9.3 **A**

You need to know the relationship between these ratios.

Return on investment = net profit margin × asset turnover

Thus

Net profit margin = return on investment ÷ asset turnover
             = 18% ÷ 2
             = 9%.

9.4 **C**

A flexible budgets have no upper limit and therefore they do not act as a cap
B the original budget is adjusted for actual activity, not costs
C resource efficiency is controlled as the amount of resource used is only allowed to increase with activity levels
D activity levels will be flexed and therefore do not act as a target.

9.5 **C**

Remember that the current ratio is current assets ÷ current liabilities.

Here the only liabilities seem to be creditors = £144,000

Current assets must be 1.7 × 144,000 = 244,800

Bank must be 244,800 − 14,800 − 19,600 = 210,400.

9.6 **A**

You need to know the relationship between these ratios.

Return on investment = net profit margin × asset turnover
             = 16% × 0.9
             = 14.4%.

9.7 **C**

This is the definition of the term "goal congruence": the alignment of goals.

9.8 **D**

(i) Flexible budgets ensure that resource usage does not rise disproportionately with activity, that is it does control efficiency.

(ii) Incremental budgeting does not look at extra units; it allows for an increment on previous budgets.

(iii) Participative budgeting is bottom up: it encourages input from more junior staff.

9.9 Some examples of a budget not producing the desired outcomes are shown below.

The manager of a production line can cut costs and hence improve its reported performances by reducing quality controls. This may result in long-term problems concerning failure of products in service, loss of customer goodwill and rectification costs.

Managers may come to consider the budget as a sum of money that has to be spent. This arises particularly in service departments or public sector organisations, the performance of which is gauged mainly through comparison of actual and budget spending.

Managers have an incentive to negotiate a budget that is not difficult to achieve. This produces a phenomenon known as "padding the budget" or "budgetary slack". A manager will exaggerate the costs required to achieve objectives.

If a manager perceives that his department's performance is falling below budget then he may sift through the costs charged to his department and demand that some be reclassified and charged elsewhere. The time and energy that goes into this kind of exercise has to be diverted from that available for the regular management of the business.

When the performance of a manager is assessed by his ability to meet budget, then he is likely to adopt a conservative approach to new business opportunities that appear. The immediate impact of new business ventures is likely to be a rise in capital and operating costs – with an adverse impact on current period profit. The benefits of such ventures may only be felt in the long term.

9.10 The qualities of a good budgetary control report are below.

Timely. The information should be made available as soon as possible after the end of the control period. Corrective action will be much more effective if it is taken soon after the event.

Accurate. Inaccurate control information could lead to inappropriate management action. There is often a conflict between the need for timeliness and the need for accuracy. The design of budgetary reporting systems should allow for sufficient accuracy for the purpose to be fulfilled.

Relevant. Busy managers should not be swamped with information that is not relevant to them. They should not need to search through a lot of irrelevant information to reach the part that relates to their area of responsibility.

Targeted. Control information should be directed to the manager who has the responsibility and authority to act upon it. If the information is communicated to the wrong manager its value will be immediately lost.

Understandable. Reports need to be understood by the person they are targeted at, this means avoidance of jargon and irrelevant information. Exception reporting may be used to keep the report clear from clutter.

9.11 A good monthly management-accounting report will have the following properties.

It will cover a range of predetermined financial performance measures, including budgets, standards and other financial requirements.

It will include aspects of non-financial performance such as service improvement targets and absenteeism.

It will direct attention to significant variations and to events that could produce significant deviations in the future.

It will represent the combination of very short-term reports available and of informal information systems, and should ensure that the manager directly involved can anticipate results.

It will act as an agenda, a way of structuring regular discussion of results, progress and plans, providing an overall view of all the activities.

9.12 The main benefits of involving managers in the budget-setting process include

- *Goal congruence.* The manager sees their organisational target as a personal target because, by their setting it, they believe it to be achievable.
- *Motivation.* The manager will be motivated to achieve the target, because not to do so would be a personal failure.
- *Accuracy/detail.* The manager will have the detailed knowledge to prepare a budget that accurately identifies the resource requirements needed to achieve the target set.

9.13 (a) Clearly those costs that have a variable element need to be flexed before they are compared to actual. Each cost will be dealt with in turn and then a budgetary control statement will be produced.

Cleaning materials, steel and other direct materials are variable and can be flexed by multiplying by $11,320 \div 9,000$.

Analyse budget cost of direct labour:

	$
9,000 hours total cost	29,000
Fixed cost	(4,250)
Therefore variable cost of 9,000 hours	24,750

$$\text{Variable cost per hour} = \frac{\$24,750}{9,000} = \$2.75$$

Therefore,

Budget cost of 11,320 hours:	$
Variable (11,320 × $2.75)	31,130
Fixed	4,250
	35,380

Use high/low technique to analyse production overheads (ignore 14,000 hours activity level to eliminate the effect of the step fixed cost):

	Hours	$
High	7,000	24,500
Low	(3,000)	(13,500)
Difference	4,000	11,000

$$\text{Variable cost} = \frac{\$11.000}{4,000 \text{ hours}} = 2.75/\text{hour}$$

	$
Variable cost of 14,000 hours (14,000 × $2.75)	= 38,500
Total cost of 14,000 hours	= 45,800
Fixed cost (for activity levels above 10,000 hours) =	7,300

	Original budget	Flexed budget	Actual	Variance
Number of machine hours	9,000	11,320	11,320	
	$	$	$	$
Cleaning materials	1,350	1,698	1,740	42 (A)
Steel	45,000	56,600	56,000	600 (F)
Other direct materials	450	566	700	134 (A)
Direct labour	29,000	35,380	32,400	2,980 (F)
Production overheads	30,000	38,430	42,600	4,170 (A)
Totals	105,800	132,674	133,440	766 (A)

(b) (i) An incremental budgeting system is a system whereby budgets are prepared by adjusting the previous period's budget/actual values for expected changes in the level of activity and for expected price changes.

A zero-based budgeting system is a system whereby all proposed activities have to be justified. Once the activity itself has been justified, then the method of carrying out the activity needs to be considered and the chosen method justified on a cost–benefit basis.

(ii) R plc is an engineering company that operates in the repairs and maintenance sector of engineering.

This type of business has difficulty in predicting the exact nature of its customers' requirements as this depends on their needs in response to machinery failures.

For R plc and similar organisations to introduce zero-based budgeting, assumptions would have to be made as to the exact nature of the customer requirements. If these assumptions were to differ significantly from the actual customer requirements, the budget would be invalid.

Budgeting: Supporting Techniques

Budgeting: Supporting Techniques

10

High–low estimation

Used to split a value into a fixed and variable element. This is most commonly used to split costs – fixed and variable.

Steps for costs,

- use past results to identify output and costs over a period
- choose the highest and lowest output levels, with associated costs
- take the difference between highest and lowest outputs and costs
    - this gives the variable costs
- divide variable costs by the extra units
    - this gives variable cost per unit
- deduct variable costs from total costs to get fixed costs.

Linear regression

This can be used in the same situations as high–low, but is deemed more reliable since it uses all the data.

In particular it can be used to form a relationship between x and y of the form

$$y = a + bx$$

where y depends on x and the relationship is believed to be linear.

In this case "a" is a fixed part of y and "b" is the variable part.

Again the most common example is the estimation of costs where

x = number of units
y = total cost (this depends on x – the number of units)
a = fixed cost
b = variable cost per unit

but other situations can be covered.

Time series

A series of figures spread over a period of time, most commonly sales.

If a pattern can be found in figures from the past then this can be continued into the future as a forecast.

Time series are split into four parts.

(Long-term) trend (T)

The long-term directional movement in the underlying series: for sales of most goods this would be upwards, but for some (typewriters and vinyl records for example) it may be downwards.

Cyclical variations (C)

Long-term fluctuations around the trend, for example fluctuations in sales caused by the trade cycle (booms and recessions).

Seasonal variations (S)

Short-term fluctuations around the trend, for example fluctuations in sales caused by Christmas. Note that this can be any fluctuation of less than one year (e.g. weekly commuter traffic on a bridge).

Random variations (R)

Fluctuations in the series caused by random and unpredictable factors; examples for sales include strikes, terrorist attacks, hurricanes, etc.

Time series come in several forms, the most common of which are the additive model where

$$\text{Time series} = T + S + C + R \text{ (for calculations we use just } T + S)$$

and the multiplicative model, where

$$\text{Time series} = T \times S \times C \times R \text{ (for calculations we use just } T \times S)$$

In this case S, C and R need to be expressed as index numbers.

The trend is most often estimated using moving averages or regression (above). Seasonal variations are estimated by averaging deviations from the trend.

? Questions

10.1 A company has used linear regression to establish a trend line of sales. It has used monthly data from January 20X1 (Period 1) until December 20X3 (Period 36) to establish trend sales (in units) as

$$y = 93{,}500 + 75x$$

The seasonal variation for January has an index value of 96.1.

Assuming that the company is using the multiplicative model to forecast sales, which of the following is closest to the forecast sales for January 20X4?

A   92,520
B   93,575
C   96,370
D   100,180

(2 marks)

10.2 AW plc is preparing its maintenance budget. The number of machine hours and maintenance costs for the past six months have been as follows:

Month	Machine hours	£
1	10,364	35,319
2	12,212	39,477
3	8,631	31,420
4	9,460	33,285
5	8,480	31,080
6	10,126	34,784

The budget cost allowance for an activity level of 9,340 machine hours, before any adjustment for price changes, is nearest to

A   £21,000
B   £30,200
C   £33,000
D   £34,300

(2 marks)

10.3 A linear regression function has been used by a company to find a link between its monthly advertising expenditure and sales (in £s). The last four years' data have been used.

An analyst has described the relationship as

$$y = 28{,}250 + 18x$$

Correlation is described as very high.

Assuming that the analysis has been done properly, which of the following statements will be substantially true?

(i)   The company has fixed advertising costs of £28,250 per month.
(ii)   Each £1 of advertising has been leading to an extra £18 of sales.
(iii)   This relationship between advertising expenditure and sales has been very strong in the past four years.

Which of these statements are substantially true?

A (i) and (ii) only
B (ii) and (iii) only
C (i) and (iii) only
D all of them

(2 marks)

10.4 The trend of a company's sales in units has been found to be represented by

$$Y = 1.8x + 250$$

where Y = sales units
x = an accounting period reference.

In accounting Period 35, the seasonal variation will have an index value of 110.

The expected sales for Period 35, to the nearest unit, are

A 285 units
B 313 units
C 319 units
D 344 units

(2 marks)

10.5 A company has used linear regression to calculate trend sales of its products. Quarterly data from the last three years has been used to establish the relationship (the first quarter of these years was referenced as Quarter 1).

The relationship is expressed as

$$y = 84,510 + 1,220x$$

The seasonal variation of the first quarter of each year is 120.

Assuming that the company is using the additive model to forecast sales, which of the following is closest to the forecast sales for Quarter 1 of next year?

A 99,720
B 100,490
C 119,120
D 120,440

(2 marks)

10.6 The overhead costs of RP Ltd have been found to be accurately represented by the formula:

$$y = £10,000 + £0.25x$$

where y is the monthly cost and x represents the activity level measured in machine hours.

Monthly activity levels, in machine hours, may be estimated using a combined regression analysis and time series model:

$$a = 100,000 + 30b$$

where a represents the de-seasonalised monthly activity level and b represents the month number.

In Month 240, when the seasonal index value is 108, the overhead cost (to the nearest £1,000) is expected to be

A   £35,000
B   £37,000
C   £39,000
D   £41,000

(3 marks)

The following data is to be used to answer both the subsequent questions:

A division of PLR plc operates a small private aircraft that carries passengers and small parcels for other divisions.

In the year ended 31 March 2002, it carried 1,024 passengers and 24,250 kg of small parcels. It incurred costs of £924,400.

The division has found that 70% of its total costs are variable, and that 60% of these vary with the number of passengers and the remainder varies with the weight of the parcels.

The company is now preparing its budget for the three months ending 30 September 2002 using an incremental budgeting approach. In this period it expects that all prices will be 3% higher than the average paid in the year ended 31 March 2002 and efficiency levels will be unchanged.

Activity levels are expected to be
209 passengers
7,200 kg of small parcels.

10.7   The budgeted passenger related cost (to the nearest £100) for the *three months* ending 30 September 2002 is

A   £81,600
B   £97,100
C   £100,000
D   £138,700

(2 marks)

10.8   The budgeted small parcel related cost (to the nearest £100) for the *three months* ending 30 September 2002 is

A   £64,700
B   £66,600
C   £79,200
D   £95,213

(2 marks)

10.9   M plc uses time series analysis and regression techniques to estimate future sales demand. Using these techniques, it has derived the following trend equation:

$$y = 10,000 + 4,200x$$

where y is the total sales units and x is the time period.

It has also derived the following seasonal variation index values for each of the quarters, using the multiplicative (proportional) seasonal variation model:

Quarter	Index value
1	120
2	80
3	95
4	105

The total sales units that will be forecast for time Period 33, which is the first quarter of Year 9, are

- A 138,720
- B 148,720
- C 176,320
- D 178,320

(3 marks)

10.10 Q Ltd used an incremental budgeting approach to setting its budgets for the year ending 30 June 2003.

The budget for the company's power costs was determined by analysing the past relationship between costs and activity levels and then adjusting for inflation of 6%.

The relationship between monthly cost and activity levels, before adjusting for the 6% inflation, was found to be

$$y = £(14,000 + 0.0025x^2)$$

where y = total cost
x = machine hours.

In April 2003, the number of machine hours was 1,525 and the actual cost incurred was £16,423. The total power cost variance to be reported is nearest to

- A £3,391 (A)
- B £3,391 (F)
- C £3,740 (F)
- D £4,580 (F)

(4 marks)

10.11 A company has estimated its annual cost structure to be of the form

$$y = 55,200 + 7.2x + 0.02x^2$$

where, x is the quantity produced and y is the total annual cost.

There has been inflation of 4% since this relationship was established.

Output is budgeted to be 980 units next month.

Which of the following is the closest to the estimated costs for next month?

- A 30,864
- B 32,099
- C 64,787
- D 84,723

(3 marks)

10.12 What are the limitations of the "high–low" method as a way of estimating cost behaviour?

(5 marks)

10.13 A company specialises in organising holidays to major sporting events. Define the four parts of a time series for the company's sales and give an example of each part.

(5 marks)

10.14 PMF plc is a long-established public transport operator that provides a commuter transit link between an airport and the centre of a large city.

The following data has been taken from the sales records of PMF plc for the last two years:

Number of passengers carried

Quarter	Year 1	Year 2
1	15,620	34,100
2	15,640	29,920
3	16,950	29,550
4	34,840	56,680

The trend equation for the number of passengers carried has been found to be

$$x = 10,000 + 4,200q$$

where x = number of passengers carried per quarter

q = time period (Year 1 Quarter 1: $q = 1$) (Year 1 Quarter 2: $q = 2$) (Year 2 Quarter 1: $q = 5$).

Based on data collected over the last two years, PMF plc has found that its quarterly costs have the following relationships with the number of passengers carried:

Cost item	Relationship
Premises costs	$y = 260,000$
Premises staff	$y = 65,000 + 0.5x$
Power	$y = 13,000 + 4x$
Transit staff	$y = 32,000 + 3x$
Other	$y = 9,100 + x$

where y = the cost per quarter (£)

x = number of passengers per quarter.

Requirements

(a) Using the trend equation for the number of passengers carried and the multiplicative (proportional) time series model determine the expected number of passengers to be carried in the third quarter of Year 3.

(7 marks)

(b) Explain why you think that the equation for the Transit staff cost is in the form

$$y = 32,000 + 3x$$

(3 marks)

(c) Using your answer to part (a) and the cost relationship equations, calculate for each cost item and in total, the costs expected to be incurred in the third quarter of Year 3.

(3 marks)

(d) Explain briefly why there may be differences between the actual data for the third quarter of Year 3 and the values you have predicted. Explain how you would judge whether you can have confidence in the predictions.

(7 marks)

(Total = 20 marks)

✓ Answers

10.1 **A**

The linear regression line gives trend sales (y) for a period (x). January 20X4 will have a period number of 37.

Trend value = 93,500 + 75 × 37 = 96,275

To get the predicted sales, adjust for the seasonal variation:

Sales = 96,275 × 96.1/100 = 92,520.

10.2 **C**

Using the high–low method to calculate the fixed/variable element of costs

	Hours	£
High	12,212	39,477
Low	8,480	31,080
Difference	3,732	8,397

VC per hour = £8,397 ÷ 3,732 hours = £2.25/hour

FC = total costs − VC = 31,080 − 2.25 × 8,480 = £12,000

Estimated costs = FC + VC/unit × Quantity = 12,000 + 2.25 × 9,340 = £33,015 = C

Make sure you have used the correct volume levels to calculate this, and extract the variable costs before the fixed.

10.3 **B**

The analyst should have chosen advertising expenditure as the independent variable (i.e. x) and sales as the dependent variable (i.e. y).

Thus sales = £28,250 + 18x (amount spent on advertising)

(i)   There is no mention of costs at all here (the £28,250 is the sales we would get with no advertising: i.e. fixed sales).

(ii) Exactly right.

(iii) This is indicated by the high correlation.

10.4 **D**

You need to calculate the trend and seasonal variation separately and combine them.

Note that the seasonal variation is described as an index number implying that the multiplicative model is being used. Note that index values are effectively percentages.

Trend = 1.8 × 35 + 250 = 313

Adjusting for seasonal variation = 313 × 110% = 344 units.

10.5 **B**

The linear regression line gives trend sales (y) for a period (x). Q1 Year 4 will have a period number of 13.

Trend value = 84,510 + 1,220 × 13 = 100,370

To get the predicted sales, adjust for the seasonal variation:

Sales = 100,370 + 120 = 100,490.

10.6 **C**

You need to forecast the machine hours so that you can then forecast the cost.

You will need to calculate the trend (de-seasonal value) and seasonal variation for the hours separately and combine them.

Note that the seasonal variation is described as an index number, implying that the multiplicative model is being used. Note that index values are effectively percentages.

Trend, a = 100,000 + 30 × 240 = 107,200 hours

Adjusting for seasonal variation = 107,200 × 108% = 115,776 hours

Total cost is therefore forecast as = 10,000 + 0.25 × 115,776 = £38,944 = C.

10.7 **A**

We need to split the costs into fixed and variable elements, adjust them to the specified activity levels and then add an increment.

	£
Variable costs (70% × £924,400)	647,080
Fixed costs (£924,400 − £647,080)	277,320

Costs varying with passengers = 60% × £647,080 = £388,248
      That is, £388,248 ÷ 1,024 = £379.15 per passenger

Costs varying with parcel weight = £647,080 − £388,248 = £258,832
      That is, £258,832 ÷ 24,250 = £10.67 per kg of parcel

Budget passenger costs = £379.15 × 209 = £79,242 before inflation
Including inflation = £79,242 × 1.03 = £81,619 = A.

10.8 **C**

Budget parcel costs = £10.67 × 7,200 = £76,824 before inflation
Including inflation = £76,824 × 1.03 = £79,129 = C.

10.9 **D**

You need to calculate the trend and seasonal variation separately and combine them.

Note that the seasonal variation is described as an index number, implying that the multiplicative model is being used. Also note that index values are effectively percentages.

Trend = 10,000 + 4,200 × 33 = £148,600

Adjusting for seasonal variation = £148,600 × 120% = £178,320.

10.10 **D**

Unusually the cost is proportional to the square of the number of hours.

First, we need to estimate the cost using the formula and then adjust for inflation.

Expected cost (before inflation) = $14,000 + 0.0025 × 1,525^2$ = £19,814

	£
Adjusting for inflation (£19,814 × 1.06)	21,003
Actual cost	16,423
Variance	4,580 = D

Note: Remember to do all calculations in the normal arithmetic order: brackets, exponentials (powers), division, multiplication, addition, subtraction.

Here there are no brackets so we square first, $1,525^2 = 2,325,625$

There is no division so we multiply next, 0.0025 × 2,325,625 = 5,814

Finally the addition, 14,000 + 5,814 = 19,814.

It is worth noting that a scientific calculator will automatically do this calculation in this order if you simply enter the figures in the order given.

10.11 **B**

The first term in the equation is clearly a fixed cost (there is no "x"), this needs to be divided by 12 to get the monthly cost.

Thus, costs (before inflation) are estimated as

$4,600 + 7.2 × 980 + 0.02 × 980^2$

= 30,864 (notice the order of calculation)

Adjusting for inflation gives

= 30,864 × 1.04

= 32,099

10.12 The limitations of the "high–low" method are shown below.

The relationship between costs and volumes is assumed to be linear, this may well not be the case for some costs.

Fixed costs are assumed to be absolutely fixed, however some fixed costs have a "step" in them.

It uses past information as a guide to the future but the nature of the relationship may change.

The most extreme past data is used to establish a relationship (highest and lowest output levels); these may be untypical.

Factors other than volume have an impact on costs (e.g. the weather will affect the heating bill); this will be ignored.

10.13 For a sport-based holiday company the pattern of its sales would incorporate the following.

(Long-term) trend. The long-term directional movement in the underlying series: for holidays this is likely to be upwards.

Cyclical variations. Long-term fluctuations around the trend, for example fluctuations in sales caused by the Olympic Games and the football World Cup (both every four years).

Seasonal variations. Short-term fluctuations around the trend, for example fluctuations in sales caused by the summer sporting calendar and people's preference for summer holidays.

Random variations. Fluctuations in the series caused by random and unpredictable factors such as strikes and terrorist attacks.

10.14 (a) The expected number of passengers can be calculated by estimating the trend and seasonal variations and combining them.

The trend can be found directly from the regression line given, and the seasonal variation will need to be estimated from the seasonal variations of the previous years.

Q3	*Trend*	*Actual*	*Seasonal variation*
Year 1	$10,000 + 4,200 \times 3 = 22,600$	16,950	$16,950 \div 22,600 = 0.75$
Year 2	$10,000 + 4,200 \times 7 = 39,400$	29,550	$29,550 \div 39,400 = 0.75$

Prediction

Trend $= 10,000 + 4,200 \times 11 = 56,200$
Seasonal variation $= 75\%$

Predicted passengers $= 56,200 \times 75\% = 42,150$.

(b) Total costs are often taken to be of the form: fixed costs + variable costs.

The equation here has a fixed cost element of £32,000. This is independent of the number of passengers carried and will comprise costs such as staff salaries. These have to be paid regardless of the activity level.

The variable cost element is £3 per passenger. This indicates that costs increase by an average of £3 for each extra passenger carried in a quarter. Note that this is an average: it is unlikely that costs increase by exactly £3 for each passenger, rather that general increases in passenger levels lead to greater employment and extra overtime.

More generally, the regression line takes this form because linear regression has been used. The underlying assumption has been that transit costs have an absolutely fixed component and a linearly variable component. The regression simply finds the straight line of best fit, even if that fit is very poor. In fact labour costs will have approximately this cost nature, although factors such as premium rate overtime will distort this.

(c)

	£
Premises	260,000
Premises staff (65,000 + 0.5 × 42,150)	86,075
Power (13,000 + 4 × 42,150)	181,600
Transit staff (32,000 + 3 × 42,150)	158,450
Other (9,100 + 42,150)	51,250
Total costs expected	737,375

(d) The actual data may be different from the above prediction for a number of reasons.

The trend may have changed due to long-term changes in society. For example the trend sales of vinyl records was upwards for many years before going into a long-term decline.

The trend may also not be linear; linear regression has been used to find the (straight) line of best fit, but it may be better represented by a curve: deviations from the prediction will then get progressively larger.

The seasonal variations may not be typical. There are only two years' data available, and although the seasonal variations are the same that may just be coincidence, or it may simply change. In addition the additive model may be a better long-term predictor.

Cyclical variations due to factors such as the trade cycle have been ignored. Clearly, air travel is significantly affected by this. If next year suffers a recession, for example, the prediction will be too high.

Random factors, by their nature, cannot be predicted. For example, a terrorist attack or major strike at the airport would significantly affect demand.

How much confidence there can be in the figures will be affected by the following.

How accurate the model has been in the past: the last eight quarters of information should be fed back into the model, and the predictions compared with the actual figures; large deviations in the past would lead to less confidence in the future.

The model should be monitored and updated, as new data becomes available the trend and seasonal variations should be revised, increasing confidence over time. Indeed confidence would increase if the data used was extended back more than two years.

Similar uses of this approach could be checked to see how accurate they are, either within this local authority's area or using data from other authorities' areas.

Organisational Structure

Organisational Structure

11

This section is a summary of some ideas that permeate the syllabus. These ideas are most commonly tested in conjunction with other areas, and form part of questions in other sections.

Organisational structure

Organisational structure relates to how the organisation fits together.

Possible structures

The most common structures are

- Entrepreneurial – small and very centralised
- Functional – split into specialist departments (marketing, finance, etc.)
- Divisional – split into autonomous business units, each containing the main functions of the business; this is usually done geographically or by product
- Matrix – split into work teams where each member reports to two (or more) managers as regards different responsibilities.

Divisionalisation

Exam questions tend to centre on this structure and concern the degree of decentralisation and its benefits.

Cost centre	Profit centre	Investment centre
←		→
Low autonomy	Medium autonomy	High autonomy
Control of costs . . . (cost decisions)	. . . and income . . . (selling price decisions)	. . . and investment (capital expenditure decisions)

Benefits

- Frees top management time to consider strategy
- Local knowledge of decision makers

- Fast decision-making
- Better performance evaluation
- Motivational improvements
- Good career path for managers.

Disadvantages

- Hard to achieve goal congruence
- Loss of control
- Decisions made by more junior staff
- Decisions may be dysfunctional
- Improved management information system needed
- Duplication.

? Questions

11.1 Why may a company adopt a product-based divisional structure over a geographical one?

(5 marks)

11.2 How would the performance of a cost centre manager be evaluated?

(5 marks)

11.3 What are the advantages of a centralised organisational structure?

(5 marks)

11.4 Why do companies adopt an organisational structure based on investment centres?

(5 marks)

✓ **Answers**

11.1 Product-based divisionalisation allows managers to specialise in a narrower range of products.

Where the products are diverse, the skills of management may only cover certain products, this will be particularly true of conglomerates with their wide range of products.

This approach may allow managers to get closer to the customers who may be interested in only certain product types.

Different product types have different risk characteristics and therefore the required return on investment may be different.

A geographical basis may be more appropriate in some situations, for example, where there are strong cultural differences amongst customers.

11.2 A manager of a cost centre will be evaluated using controllable, traceable factors, that is, costs that relate to the division that he controls.

These are likely to include staff costs (assuming the manager can hire and fire staff) but exclude head office apportioned costs.
Performance measures used could include cost per unit or total cost against (flexed) budget.

In addition costs could be compared against some indicator of size (e.g. costs per square metre for a retail unit).

Revenues and capital expenditure should be excluded as they are not controllable by the manager.

11.3 Centralised structures are often criticised for being bureaucratic, unresponsive and for stifling initiative. However, they have some advantages.

- Centralised structures are easier to control with their clear lines of command and autocratic structures.
- A centralised structure avoids the need for transfer pricing.
- Centralised organisations do not suffer from the loss of goal congruence experienced in their decentralised counterparts.
- Centralised structures avoid the duplication inherent in decentralised organisations.

11.4 An organisational structure based on investment centres represents the highest degree of decentralisation achieved by most companies, representing the situation where cost, revenue and investment decisions are made by divisional management.

This high degree of autonomy should lead to significant motivational benefits with local managers.

Giving significant powers to local managers should relieve central management of its operational obligations, allowing time for strategic considerations.

Decision-making should be faster and more relevant to local conditions when local managers have more power.

The performance of the various components of a company's operations can be evaluated separated from overall performance.

Financial
Performance
Evaluation

Financial Performance Evaluation

12

Return on investment (ROI)

Calculation

$$ROI = \frac{ProfitBeforeInterestAndTax}{CapitalEmployed}$$

This will be compared with a target, usually a company's cost of capital or an industry benchmark.

There are problems with all the three figures needed.

1 Profit

- Before tax?
- Accounting policies?
- Sharing of jointly made profits?
- Transfer pricing?

2 Capital

- Depreciate assets?
- Inflate assets?
- Capitalise leased assets?
- Shared assets?

3 Target

- Cost of capital (a cash-based measure)?
- Industry target (achievable, company differences)?

In addition return on investment can lead to dysfunctional decisions where the return on an investment is between the division's existing return and the target.

Example

Divisional existing return = 15%
Target return = 12%
New investment return = 14%

The manager will tend to reject since the investment would drag down the division's over-all return and make the manager's performance appear worse. The company wants this investment to be undertaken since it offers a return in excess of target.

Residual income (RI)

Calculation

$$RI = \text{Profit Before Interest and Tax} - \text{Target Return} \times \text{Capital Employed}$$

For good performance this is positive.

Most of the problems are the same as for return on investment, except that dysfunctional decisions should not occur.

Unfortunately residual income is not comparable between divisions (it is in £ not %).

Transfer pricing

A transfer price (TP) is an internal price used to record sales from one division to another. It splits corporate profit between the divisions.

Aims

- Goal congruence between divisions and company
- Incentives to managers to produce
- Good performance evaluation
- Divisional autonomy
- Equitable profit split.

In practice no transfer price will achieve all these aims.

Methods

Cost plus. Transfer price is set at cost plus a profit margin (NB standard cost is better than actual, marginal cost usually better than absorption cost).

Two part. Transfer price is a unit charge (usually based on marginal cost) plus a periodic charge (usually based on fixed overheads).

Negotiated. The divisions agree a transfer price between themselves.

Market. Use the open market price for the transferred good (sometimes modified by divisional cost savings).

Dual price. The selling division has a different price to the purchasing division (usually absorption cost + mark-up and marginal cost respectively).

Optimum transfer pricing

About the best TP can be found using the following (assuming A sells to B):

Division A	TP > marginal cost + opportunity cost (zero, if spare capacity)
Division B	TP < unit contribution (before transfer price) and
	TP < external price

International transfer pricing

The transfer price can be used to move profits around to minimise global tax liabilities and to repatriate profits, circumventing some currency controls.

❓ Questions

12.1 A company has set a target ROI of 12% for its divisions, this is deemed to represent the return necessary to benefit the company.

Division D achieved an ROI of 17% last year and is not expecting any major change from ongoing operations.

The purchase of a new piece of equipment has been proposed by a member of the production team. It is estimated that it will boost profits by £128,000 per annum for an investment of £855,000.

Which of the following statements represents the most likely outcome?

A   The divisional manager will undertake the investment to the benefit of the company.
B   The divisional manager will undertake the investment to the detriment of the company.
C   The divisional manager will reject the investment to the benefit of the company.
D   The divisional manager will reject the investment to the detriment of the company.

(2 marks)

12.2 A company has set a target ROI of 14% for its divisions, this is based on the company's cost of capital.

Division D achieved an ROI of 8% last year and is not expecting any major change from ongoing operations. However, a manager has suggested that cost savings of £15,000 per annum can be obtained by investing £135,000 in upgrading a particular piece of equipment.

Which of the following statements represents the most likely outcome?

A   The divisional manager will undertake the investment to the benefit of the company.
B   The divisional manager will undertake the investment to the detriment of the company.
C   The divisional manager will reject the investment to the benefit of the company.
D   The divisional manager will reject the investment to the detriment of the company.

(2 marks)

12.3 A company uses ROI to assess divisional performance, but it is considering switching to RI. The company's cost of capital is 15%.

Division C has an ROI of 21% which is not expected to change. An investment of £155,000 is available, which is expected to yield profits of £28,000 per annum.

Which of the following is the most likely decision of the manager of division C?

	ROI used to assess performance	RI used to assess performance
A	Accept	Accept
B	Accept	Reject
C	Reject	Accept
D	Reject	Reject

(2 marks)

12.4 Division G of a large company is approaching its year end. The division is evaluated using ROI with a target rate of return of 15%. The division has control of all aspects of its operation except that all cash balances are centralised by the company and therefore left off divisional balance sheets.

The divisional manager is considering the following options.

(i) To delay payment of a supplier until next year, the potential prompt payment discount of 5% will be lost. The debt is for £27,500.

(ii) To scrap a redundant asset with a book value of £147,000. The manager has been offered £15,000 as immediate scrap proceeds, whilst he is fairly confident that he could get £25,000 in an industry auction to be held at the start of the new year.

Assume that the manager is very short-termist (i.e. only considers the implications for this year) and that the expected ROI for the year, before these options, is 18%.

Which of the following represents the most likely combination that the manager will choose?

	(i)	(ii)
A	Delay	Scrap now
B	Delay	Scrap next year
C	Do not delay	Scrap now
D	Do not delay	Scrap next year

(2 marks)

Use the following information to answer the next two questions.

A divisionalised company uses transfer pricing as part of its management information system. Each manager is assessed on their divisional profit.

Division A makes a unit for £10 variable cost and £3 of fixed cost is absorbed.
Division B takes these units, incurs another £8 variable cost and absorbs £4.
It then sells them for £21.
The transfer price is set at £12.

There are no capacity constraints and all fixed costs are unavoidable in the short run.

12.5 Which of the following represents the most likely course of action that each divisional manager wishes to pursue?

	Manager A	Manager B
A	Produce	Produce
B	Produce	Not produce
C	Not produce	Produce
D	Not produce	Not produce

(2 marks)

12.6   Which of the following best represents the company's position?

A   Production should occur and the TP is goal congruent
B   Production should occur and the TP is not goal congruent
C   Production should not occur and the TP is goal congruent
D   Production should not occur and the TP is not goal congruent

(2 marks)

12.7   A company makes widgets in two stages, handled by divisions A and B. A transfer price is used to record movements of partially completed widgets from A to B.

The TP is set at the actual variable cost of A + 25%.

Information regarding the divisions is shown below.

	Division A		*Division B*
Standard cost	£40	Standard cost	£20
Actual cost	£48	Actual cost	£18
		Selling price	£100

Actual and budget volume was 1,000 widgets. The selling price was as anticipated.

Which of the following statements best represents the measured performance of the two divisions, according to the company's system?

	Division A	*Division B*
A	Profit above budget	Profit above budget
B	Profit above budget	Profit below budget
C	Profit below budget	Profit above budget
D	Profit below budget	Profit below budget

(3 marks)

12.8   A company has set a target ROI of 14% for its divisions, this is based on the company's cost of capital.

Division X has had an ROI of 18% for some years and is not expecting any major change from ongoing operations. The divisional manager is contemplating scrapping an old pieceof equipment with a book value of £44,000 which yields only £7,000 per annum in profits.

Which of the following statements represents the most likely choice of the manager?

A   The divisional manager will scrap the equipment to the benefit of the company.
B   The divisional manager will scrap the equipment to the detriment of the company.
C   The divisional manager will not scrap the equipment to the benefit of the company.
D   The divisional manager will not scrap the equipment to the detriment of the company.

(2 marks)

12.9   A company is experimenting with both ROI and RI to assess divisional performance. In both cases a target return of 12% is used.

Division R has net assets of £875,200 with profits of £175,000. These figures are before adjusting for what is below.

A manager is considering scrapping some equipment with a book value of £145,000. The equipment only yields £12,000 of profit per year. The equipment contains several industrial pollutants and the *cost* of scrapping it will be £25,000.

Assume that the manager only considers the impact on this year's performance.

Which of the following is the best description of the likely actions of the manager?

	ROI used to assess performance	*RI used to assess performance*
A	Accept	Accept
B	Accept	Reject
C	Reject	Accept
D	Reject	Reject

(3 marks)

12.10   Which of the following is NOT a method of transfer pricing?

   A   Cost plus transfer price
   B   Internal price transfer price
   C   Market-based transfer price
   D   Two part transfer price.

(2 marks)

Use the following information to answer the next two questions.

Division A of a company makes units which are then transferred to other divisions.

There is a competitive intermediate market for these units, with a price of £15 per unit. Division A then incurs a selling cost of £2.
Variable production cost = £7 per unit and fixed cost = £3 per unit.

12.11   Assume the division has spare capacity.

   Which of the following is the minimum TP that will encourage the divisional manager of A to transfer units to other divisions?

   A   £7.01
   B   £10.01
   C   £13.01
   D   £15.01

(2 marks)

12.12   Assume the division has no spare capacity.

   Which of the following is the minimum TP that will encourage the divisional manager of A to transfer units to other divisions?

   A   £7.01
   B   £10.01
   C   £13.01
   D   £15.01

(2 marks)

Use the following information to answer the next two questions.

A company makes widgets in two stages, handled by divisions A and B. A transfer price of £54 is used to record movements of partially completed widgets between the divisions.

Division A makes a widget for £45 variable cost and £11 of fixed cost is absorbed.

Division B then incurs another £27 variable cost and absorbs £14. It then sells them for £80.

There are no capacity constraints and all fixed costs are unavoidable in the short run.

12.13 Which of the following represents the most likely course of action that each divisional manager wishes to pursue?

	Manager A	Manager B
A	Produce	Produce
B	Produce	Not produce
C	Not produce	Produce
D	Not produce	Not produce

(2 marks)

12.14 Which of the following best represents the company's position?

A Production should occur and the TP is goal congruent
B Production should occur and the TP is not goal congruent
C Production should not occur and the TP is goal congruent
D Production should not occur and the TP is not goal congruent

(2 marks)

12.15 TM plc makes components which it sells internally to its subsidiary RM Ltd, as well as to its own external market.

The external market price is £24.00 per unit, which yields a contribution of 40% of sales. For external sales, variable costs include £1.50 per unit for distribution costs, which are not incurred on internal sales.

TM plc has sufficient capacity to meet all of the internal and external sales. In order to maximise group profit, the component should be transferred to RM Ltd at a price for each unit of

A £24.00
B £22.50
C £14.40
D £12.90

(2 marks)

12.16 A company calculates EVA® on divisional performance. The following information relates to division X.

Operating profit	£35m
Depreciation	£18m
R & D expenditure	£12m
Advertising expenditure	£10m
Required return	12%
Capital employed	£98m

The R & D was written off as incurred. The product being developed has an expected life of 4 years.

The advertising expenditure related 50% to this year and 50% to a campaign starting shortly after the year-end.

Which of the following is likely to be closest to division X's EVA®?

Ignore taxation.

A £39.8m
B £37.2m
C £30.8m
D £22.8m

(2 marks)

12.17 Division A makes alphas which are converted into betas by division B. A's variable costs are £150 per unit and B's are £80 per unit. B sells completed betas for £290 each.

There is an intermediate market for alphas with a price of £180 which significantly exceeds the capacity of divisions A and B.

(i) Assuming that B cannot buy from the market in alphas (but A can sell into the market), what is the widest range of TP that encourages the divisions to trade with each other?

(ii) Assuming that A cannot sell into the market in alphas (but B can buy from the market), what is the widest range of TP that now encourages the divisions to trade with each other?

(5 marks)

12.18 A company has 2 divisions which contribute to the production and sales of widgets: division A produces them and transfers them to division B which sells them.

Division A incurs variable costs of £15,200 per unit and monthly fixed costs of £10,700.

Division B incurs variable costs of £7,500 per unit and monthly fixed costs of £3,400.

Division B faces the following monthly demand for the widgets.

Demand	Price
1	£60,000
2	£55,000
3	£50,000
4	£45,000
5	£40,000
6	£35,000
7	£30,000

The transfer price (TP) between the divisions has been set at £25,000.

Explain the likely effects of this TP and suggest an alternative.

(5 marks)

12.19 MCP plc specialises in providing marketing, data collection, data processing and consulting services. The company is divided into divisions that provide services to each other and also to external clients. The performance of the Divisional Managers is measured against profit targets that are set by central management.

During October, the Consulting division undertook a project for AX plc. The agreed fee was £15,500 and the costs excluding data processing were £2,600. The data processing, which needed 200 hours of processing time, was carried out by the Data Processing (DP) division. An external agency could have been used to do the data processing, but the DP division had 200 chargeable skilled hours available in October.

The DP division provides DP services to the other divisions and also to external customers. The budgeted costs of the DP division for the year ending 31 December 2002, which is divided into 12 equal monthly periods, are as follows:

Variable costs

	£
Skilled labour (6,000 hours worked)	216,000
Other processing costs	60,000
Fixed costs	240,000

These costs are recovered on the basis of chargeable skilled labour hours (data processing hours) which are budgeted to be 90% of skilled labour hours worked. The DP division's external pricing policy is to add a 40% mark-up to its total budgeted cost per chargeable hour.

During October 2002, actual labour costs incurred by the DP division were 10% higher than expected, but other costs were 5% lower than expected.

Requirements

(a) Calculate the total transfer value that would have been charged by the DP division to the Consulting division for the 200 hours on its AX plc project, using the following bases:

   (i)   actual variable cost
   (ii) standard variable cost + 40% mark-up
   (iii) market price.

(6 marks)

(b) Calculate the budgeted profit for this project using the alternative values calculated in answer to requirement (a) for each of the DP division *and* the Consulting division *and* in total.

(9 marks)

(c) Recommend the transfer value that should be used for the 200 hours of processing time in October. Your answer need not be one of those calculated in your answer to requirement (a) above.

(5 marks)
(Total = 20 marks)

12.20 XYZ motor group comprises three autonomous divisions and its divisional managers are paid salary bonuses linked to the profit that their respective divisions achieve.

The New Vehicle (NV) division has a city showroom. It sells new vehicles and accepts trade-ins which are sold to the Used Vehicle (UV) division at a 'going trade price' less any necessary repair costs. The Vehicle Repair (VR) division performs necessary repair work to trade-ins and invoices UV for such work on a full cost plus basis. Both the UV and VR divisions do a great deal of business unrelated to trade-ins.

NV has the option of selling a new vehicle to a customer for £40,000 (including a 25% profit mark up on cost) providing the customer is given a trade-in value of £28,000 on his old vehicle. Reference to used car value guides indicate that the going trade price for the trade-in vehicle will be £17,500. However, it is estimated that UV division will be able to sell the trade in for £28,900 after incurring a charge from VR for repairing the vehicle as follows:

	£
Variable costs	500
Fixed overheads	250 (being 50% of VCs)
Mark up	75 (being 10% on cost)
Total	825

Requirements

(a) Calculate the impact on the contribution of each division and XYZ in total of proceeding with the new car sale on the terms specified

(10 marks)

(b) Explain the possible sources of conflict between the managers of the three divisions and the XYZ group management arising from the organisational arrangement of the XYZ group and its transfer pricing system

(8 marks)

(c) Having regard to your answers to (a) and (b) propose any modifications to the transfer pricing system that your consider appropriate

(7 marks)

Note: the 'trade price' for a used vehicle is the price at which one car dealer would sell a vehicle to another dealer without warranties or guarantees

(Total = 25 marks)

☑ Answers

12.1 **D**

The ROI of the investment is £128,000 ÷ £855,000 = 15%.

Thus the manager's performance will appear to decline if he takes on this project (his new return will fall below the existing 17%). He will therefore reject this investment.

However, a return of 15% is beneficial to the company, and so the manager rejects to the detriment of the company.

12.2 **B**

The ROI of the investment is £15,000 ÷ £135,000 = 11%.

Thus the manager's performance will appear to improve if he takes on this project (his new return will rise above the existing 8%). He will therefore accept this investment.

However, a return of 11% is detrimental to the company, and so the manager accepts to the detriment of the company.

12.3 **C**

The ROI of the investment is £28,000 ÷ £155,000 = 18%.

This will reduce the division's ROI and will cause the manager to reject.

The RI is £28,000 − 15% × £155,000 = £4,750.

Since this is positive the manager will accept.

12.4 **A**

It is worth noting that you do not need the figures to work this question out (although you can use them if you want).

(i) Paying now would reduce creditors and thus increase capital employed, leading to lower rates of return. Note that the "return" of 5% is nowhere near high enough to make this worth considering.

(ii) Scrapping will reduce the capital employed, leading to higher returns, the income will just accentuate this.

12.5 **A**

Each manager will only consider costs that are variable to him, fixed costs will be ignored – they are unavoidable.

Manager A will want to produce as the transfer price (£12) exceeds his variable cost (£10), adding to his contribution.

Manager B will want to produce as the revenue from the sale (£21) exceeds the variable cost and transfer price (£8 + £12), adding to his contribution.

12.6 **A**

The company will increase its contribution if production occurs, because the final selling price is greater than the total variable costs.

The position is goal congruent since both divisions wish to produce.

12.7 **B**

Remember that the divisional performance will depend on the TP, which will increase due to A's poor performance.

We will do the calculation for one unit, although you could do it for 1,000 if you preferred.

Budget TP = £40 + 25% = £50
Actual TP = £48 + 25% = £60

A's budget profit is £50 − £40 = £10 per unit
A's actual profit is £60 − £48 = £12 per unit – above budget

B's budget profit is £100 − £20 − £50 = £30 per unit
B's actual profit is £100 − £18 − £60 = £22 per unit – below budget.

12.8 **B**

The ROI of the equipment is £7,000 ÷ £44,000 = 16%

Thus, the manager's performance will appear to improve if he scraps the equipment (his new return will rise above the existing 18%).

However, a return of 16% is beneficial to the company, and so the manager should not scrap the asset.

12.9 D

You can do this by just looking at the ROI separately, but it can be quite hard to see how a divestment decision affects overall returns. So we have simply worked out the old and new ROI. Similarly for RI.

The division's current ROI = £175,000 ÷ £875,200 = 20%

The new ROI = (£175,000 − £12,000 − £25,000) ÷ (£875,200 − £145,000) = 19%

The current RI = £175,000 − 12% × £875,200 = £69,976

The new RI = (£175,000 − £12,000 − £25,000) − 12% × (£875,200 − £145,000) = £50,376

Since both ROI and RI have fallen the manager will reject under both performance appraisal systems.

12.10 B

The internal price is just another name for the TP, so it is not a method of transfer pricing.

12.11 A

Any price above variable cost will generate a positive contribution, and will therefore be accepted.

12.12 C

The division will need to give up a unit sold externally in order to make a transfer, this is only worthwhile if the income of a transfer is greater than the *net* income of an external sale.

12.13 B

Each manager will only consider costs that are variable to him, fixed costs will be ignored – they are unavoidable.

Manager A will want to produce as the transfer price (£54) exceeds his variable cost (£45), adding to his contribution.

Manager B will not want to produce as the revenue from the sale (£80) is exceeded by the variable cost and transfer price (£27 + £54), reducing his contribution.

12.14 B

The company will increase its contribution if production occurs, because the final selling price is greater than the total variable costs.

The position is not goal congruent since not both divisions wish to produce.

12.15 D

You must set a price high enough for TM to cover its costs, but not so high that RM cannot make a profit.

For TM, an item sold externally has VC of 60% × £24.00 = £14.40

Of this, £1.50 will not be incurred on an internal transfer so it is not relevant here, VC on internal transfer = £14.40 − £1.50 = £12.90

We do not know RM's cost structure, so we leave the price at £12.90; this will ensure that RM is not discouraged from taking an internal transfer when it is profitable to do so.

12.16 **B**

EVA® is similar to residual income in that it subtracts a notional capital charge from profit to obtain a performance figure: the "economic value added".

Some changes to normal accounting procedures are used to make the figures more appropriate.

	£m
Operating profit	35
Add: R & D	12
Advertising	10
Less: 25% R & D	3
Less: 50% Advertising	5
Adjusted profit	49

EVA® = £49 m − 12% × £98 m = £37.2 m

12.17 (i) A can sell all of its output into the intermediate market at £180, so the TP needs to exceed this.

B needs to make a contribution so the TP needs to be below £290 − £80 = £210

So, £180 < TP < £210.

(ii) A needs to cover its costs, so TP must exceed £150.

B can buy from the intermediate market at £180, so the TP must be lower than this.

So, £150 < TP < £180.

12.18 Division A will want to transfer widgets as long as the TP exceeds the marginal cost (MC).

This is true for every potential unit, that is division A will transfer as many units as B will buy.

Division B will want to buy in a unit as long as the contribution (more correctly net marginal revenue, NMR) exceeds the TP.

This is investigated below:

Quantity	Price	TR	MR	MC A	MC B	MC Co	NMR B	MR > MC for co?
1	60000	60000	60000	15200	7500	22700	52500	y
2	55000	110000	50000	15200	7500	22700	42500	y
3	50000	150000	40000	15200	7500	22700	32500	y
4	45000	180000	30000	15200	7500	22700	22500	y

5	40000	200000	20000	15200	7500	22700	12500	n
6	35000	210000	10000	15200	7500	22700	2500	n
7	30000	210000	0	15200	7500	22700	−7500	n

From the above it can be seen that the company's profits are maximised at 4 units: the marginal revenue (MR) exceeds the MC for all units up to this level.

Unfortunately the TP of £25,000 will discourage division B from buying the 4th unit: it will only generate £22,500 of contribution (correctly: NMR) at a cost of £25,000.

Thus, division B will buy 3 units from A and sell them at £50,000 each.

In order that division B wants to buy exactly 4 units the TP needs to be lower than the NMR of the 4th unit but not as low as the NMR of the 5th unit.

i.e.   £12,500 < TP < £22,500

In addition, the TP must be high enough to ensure that division A still wants to produce.

i.e.   TP > £15,200

Thus, a TP in the range:

£15,200 < TP < £22,500 will achieve the company aims

e.g. set the TP at £18,000

12.19 (a)

(i) Actual variable cost

(Note that these figures are for a year but the same answer would be obtained if monthly figures were used.)

	£
Skilled labour (216,000 × 1.1)	237,600
Other processing costs (60,000 × 0.95)	57,000
	294,600
Total chargeable hours (6,000 × 0.9)	5,400
Rate (294,600 ÷ 5,400)	54.56/hour

Charge = £54.56 × 200 hours = £10,912.

(ii) Standard variable cost

	£
Skilled labour (6,000 hours worked)	216,000
Other processing costs	60,000
	276,000
Mark-up (40% × 276,000)	110,400
	386,400
Rate (386,400 ÷ 5,400)	71.56/hour

Charge = £71.56 × 200 hours = £14,312.

(iii) Market price

	£
Standard + 40% mark-up	71.56 (From above)
Fixed costs + 40% (£240,000 × 1.4 ÷ 5,400)	62.22
Market price	133.78

Charge = £133.78 × 200 hours = £26,756.

(b) Summary budgeted profit and loss statements

DP division	(i) £	(ii) £	(iii) £
Sales (transfer out)	10,912	14,312	26,756
Labour (216,000 ÷ 5,400 × 200)	(8,000)	(8,000)	(8,000)
Other (60,000 ÷ 5,400 × 200)	(2,222)	(2,222)	(2,222)
FC (240,000 ÷ 5,400 × 200)	(8,889)	(8,889)	(8,889)
Profit	(8,199)	(4,799)	7,645

Consulting division

Sales	15,500	15,500	15,500
DP (transfers in)	(10,912)	(14,312)	(26,756)
Other costs	(2,600)	(2,600)	(2,600)
Profit	1,988	(1,412)	(13,856)
Total (sum)	(6,211)	(6,211)	(6,211)

(c) The project makes an accounting loss overall, but this is only due to the absorption of fixed costs in DP division. The project therefore adds to the company's contribution and should be accepted.

Assuming that divisional managers only make decisions by considering relevant costs, the transfer price which encourages the managers to make correct decisions can be ascertained as follows.

For DP division:
$$TP > \text{marginal cost} + \text{opportunity cost}$$
i.e. TP > 8,000 + 2,222 + 0 (no opportunity cost)
i.e. TP > 10,222

For Consulting division:
$$TP < \text{net contribution}$$
i.e. TP < 15,500 − 2,600
i.e. TP < 12,900

As long as the TP is in this range both managers would want to make the transfer, say TP = £11,000.

Note that the original case (i) is in this range, yielding a positive contribution for each division.

12.20   (a)

NV (New Vehicle division)

	£
Margin on new vehicle	8,000 (40,000 × 20%)
Trade in value given	−28,000
Transfer price	−16,675 (17,500 − 825)
Total	−3,325

UV (Used Vehicle division)

	£
Sale proceeds	28,900
Repair costs	−825
Transfer price	−16,675
Total	11,400

VR (Vehicle Repair division)

	£
Repairs invoiced	825
Variable costs	−500
Total	325

XYZ Motor Group

	£
NV	−3,325
UV	11,400
VR	325
Total	8,400

(b)   Sources of conflict may possibly include any or all of the following:

- The existing system places all the benefit from the sale of used cars with UV division. In the absence of trade-ins this might be fair, but obtaining used cars as trade-ins on sale of new cars involves input from NV division. It would be equitable to allow a margin to NV division on such transactions.
- In the case study given, the decision on whether or not to accept the deal on the sale of the new £40,000 car rests with the NV division manager. Although the deal is profitable to the XYZ group, the transfer price system means that it inflicts a small loss on NV. The NV manager might turn it down.
- The system allows VR division to pass on to NV all its costs plus a generous margin for the work it does. This might encourage VR division to load costs onto transfer work and to pass on inefficiencies to other divisions.
- VR's transfer charges include both fixed and variable components with no allowance for the existence or otherwise of opportunity costs. Although not critical in the case study, such a situation may induce sub-optimal decision making when NV or UV division perceives all of the VR's charges to be fixed.

(c) The ideal or correct transfer price is the marginal cost incurred by the transferor division plus any opportunity cost suffered by that division. This (1) provides a reasonably equitable distribution of profit between the transferor and transferee division and (2) minimises the possibility of dysfunctional behaviour. However, it can be very difficult to design and operate a system that works on this principle.

One difficulty is that it can be difficult to state unambiguously what marginal cost is. The marginal cost of doing something may be different when viewed on a short-term or long-term basis. Furthermore, opportunity cost may be a very vague concept. If VR is not working to full capacity then a £500 marginal cost for the job might be a fair transfer price. But if VR is working to full capacity and has to turn away outside work offering a contribution of £325 then £825 becomes a fair transfer price for the job in question. But whether or not VR is working to full capacity at any given time may be difficult to determine with certainty. In any event, it may be possible to defer outside work rather than turn it away in order to free up some capacity. It is difficult to accommodate such an imprecise state of affairs in a structured system.

The internal transfer of used vehicles to UV division at trade price appears to be inequitable. Given NV'S contribution to the acquisition it seems fairer that the used cars be transferred at trade price plus a mark up. This would allow for the fact that many of the activities and risks normally associated with the outside purchase of a used car are avoided by UV in the case of internal transfers.

A simple and practical solution to the problems of XYZ might include the following principal system design features:

- Transfer of trade-in vehicles from NV to UV at trade price plus a mark up. The mark up should recognize the role that NV plays in obtaining the trade-in.
- Charging the cost of VR repairs to NV and UV at marginal cost plus a modest margin – unless there is a clear capacity shortage. Alternatively, VR might be required to quote for transfer work against outside competitors.

Non-financial
Performance
Evaluation

Non-financial Performance Evaluation 13

🔑 Benchmarking

Benchmarking involves setting performance targets (e.g. standards) for a business unit, based on the actual performance achieved by someone external. It can be used for financial or non-financial performance.

Clearly this will lead to targets that are hard but achievable.

Competitive benchmarking

Targets are based on the best company in a particular industry. Unfortunately data may not be easy to obtain, and even then it may not be comparable.

Internal benchmarking

The best performing division in a company is used as a target for the other divisions. This can lead to inter-divisional rivalry and conflict within the company.

Functional benchmarking

Particular business functions are compared (e.g. credit control), this is often across industries. The level of detail required can be particularly hard to obtain and the environmental conditions may be quite different.

Strategic benchmarking

Strategic methods and processes are observed in successful companies, appropriate lessons are learned and improvements implemented. This approach is clearly more general than the others and leads to less-specific improvements.

Balanced scorecard

Aims to look at both the indicators of success and determinants of future success. It looks at four "perspectives". Under each, a company should state its aims and specify measures of performance.

Some examples:

		Aims	Measures*
1	Financial perspective	Profitability	ROI
		Survival	Current ratio
2	Customer perspective	Satisfaction	Returning customers
		Quality	Defect rate
3	Internal business perspective	Staff motivation	Absenteeism
		Efficiency	Throughput rates
4	Innovation and learning perspective	New products	Income from new products
		Learning	Employee suggestions adopted

* It is generally considered best practice to use ratios rather than absolute figures.

? Questions

13.1 A company wishes to encourage divisions to improve profitability and reduce the defect rate of production. With this aim the following formula is used to assess performance, with a target for p of 10%.

$$p = r - 2d$$

where,
p = performance
r = return on investment
d = defect rate

Note: All figures are percentages.

Currently division S has investment of £340,000 with profit of £68,000 and a defect rate of 3%.

Spending £120,000 on new equipment is expected to reduce the defect rate and slightly increase profits by £7,900.

Which of the following is the closest to the condition that is likely to lead to the manager buying the equipment?

A The new defect rate must be less than 1.25%.
B The new defect rate must be less than 1.75%.
C The new defect rate must be less than 4.75%.
D The manager will never buy the equipment.

(4 marks)

13.2 The following statements compare internal benchmarking to competitive benchmarking.

   (i) Internal benchmarking can lead to relatively high levels of inter-divisional conflict.

   (ii) It is relatively hard to source non-financial information for use with internal benchmarking.

   Which of the following is the best description of the truth of these two statements?

	(i)	(ii)
A	True	True
B	True	False
C	False	True
D	False	False

   (2 marks)

13.3 Which of the following is not a form of benchmarking?

   A   Best practice benchmarking
   B   Competitive benchmarking
   C   Internal benchmarking
   D   Functional benchmarking

   (2 marks)

13.4 A bus company wishes to encourage its regional managers to improve profitability and reliability. With this aim the following formula is used to assess performance, with a target for π of 6%.

   $$\pi = n - 30d$$

   where,
   π = performance
   n = net profit margin
   d = delayed journey rate (% of journeys delayed or cancelled)

   Note: All figures are percentages.

   Currently northern region has sales of £17,500,000, profits of £3,500,000 and a delayed journey rate of 0.5%.

   Employing extra staff on standby at the depots would be expected to reduce the delayed journey rate to 0.4%, but lead to no extra sales income.

   Which of the following is the closest to the condition that is likely to lead to the manager employing the extra staff?

   A   The cost is less than £350,000
   B   The cost is less than £525,000
   C   The cost is less than £2,975,000
   D   The manager will not employ extra staff

   (4 marks)

13.5 Which of the following is NOT one of the headings on a balanced scorecard?

    A   The financial perspective
    B   The customer perspective
    C   The employee perspective
    D   The innovation and learning perspective

(2 marks)

13.6 Why are financial performance indicators not considered sufficient for measuring the performance of part of an organisation?

(5 marks)

13.7 Explain what is meant by the "internal business perspective" of the balanced scorecard and give some examples of measures that could be used for a private hospital.

(5 marks)

13.8 Give an example of a ratio for each of the components of a balanced score card for a mobile phone (service provider) company.

(5 marks)

13.9 CM Ltd was formed 10 years ago to provide business equipment solutions to local businesses. It has separate divisions for research, marketing, product design, technology and communication services, and now manufactures and supplies a wide range of business equipment (copiers, scanners, printers, fax machines and similar items).

To date it has evaluated its performance using monthly financial reports that analyse profitability by type of equipment.

The Managing Director of CM Ltd has recently returned from a course on which it had been suggested that the "Balanced Scorecard" could be a useful way of measuring performance.

Requirements

(a)   Explain the "Balanced Scorecard" and how it could be used by CM Ltd to measure its performance.

(10 marks)

While on the course, the Managing Director of CM Ltd overheard someone mention how the performance of their company had improved after they introduced "Benchmarking".

(b)   Explain "Benchmarking" and how it could be used to improve the performance of CM Ltd.

(10 marks)
(Total = 20 marks)

✅ Answers

13.1 **A**

We need to find out the current value of p and then ensure that it rises with this purchase of equipment.

Current p = £68,000 ÷ £340,000 − 2 × 3% = 14%

New p (assuming no change to the defect rate)
$$(£68,000 + £7,900) ÷ (£340,000 + £120,000) - 2 × 3\% = 10.5\%$$

For the manager to buy this equipment this value must increase by
$$14\% - 10.5\% = 3.5\%$$

Thus the defect rate must fall by half of this, that is, 1.75%
So the rate is $3\% - 1.75\% = 1.25\%$.

Alternatively, use algebra:
$$(£68,000 + £7,900) ÷ (£340,000 + £120,000) - 2d = 0.14$$
solve to give $d = 0.0125$.

13.2 **B**

(i) Divisions are being compared with each other which makes them rivals.
(ii) It is generally much easier to find information for internal benchmarking since competitors try to protect their sensitive information.

13.3 **A**

Finding the best practice is what benchmarking is all about, it is not a form of benchmarking. All the others tell you where the benchmark is from.

13.4 **B**

Note that the extra staff have two effects: an increase in costs (with a consequent fall in margin) and a reduction in the delayed journey rate. We need to ensure that the fall in the delayed journey rate more than offsets the increase in costs.

(Working in £'000)
Profit margin $= 3,500 ÷ 17,500 = 20\%$
Current $\pi = 20\% - 30 × 0.5\% = 5\%$

New π (assuming no change to costs) $= 20\% - 30 × 0.4\% = 8\%$

Thus the profit margin could fall by $8\% - 5\% = 3\%$ and the manager would be no worse off (i.e. margin could fall to 17%).

A margin of 17% implies profits of $17\% × 17,500 = 2,975$
Costs could increase by $3,500 - 2,975 = 525$

Alternatively, use algebra.

13.5 **C**

The employee perspective should be the internal business perspective (this will cover employee issues, but is much wider than that).

13.6 Financial performance indicators are not considered sufficient for measuring the performance of part of an organisation for the following reasons:

They focus on whether success has been achieved rather than whether success is likely to be achieved in the future.

They only tell you what has happened over a limited period in the immediate past.

They give you no indication of what is going to happen in the future, the range of possibilities or their determinants.

They are vulnerable to manipulation and to the choice of accounting policy on matters such as depreciation and stock valuation.

They do not relate to the strategic management of the business and may induce "short-termism".

13.7 The internal business perspective of the balanced scorecard refers to a company's internal efficiency. It includes the ability to obtain, retain and efficiently use resources.

The following are some examples of measures.

Staff turnover, the proportion of staff leaving each period.
Absenteeism, the proportion of staff not attending work.
Bed occupancy rates showing how well the wards are being utilised.
Surgeon productive hours, probably as a percentage of total hours to show the efficient use of skilled worker time.

13.8 Financial perspective: return on capital employed.

Customer perspective: churn rate (number of customers not renewing their subscription).

Internal business perspective: staff turnover.

Innovation and learning perspective: percentage of customers on new tariffs.

13.9 (a) The balanced scorecard is an attempt to extend performance evaluation beyond purely financial areas (which simply measure whether a company has been successful) to include important non-financial areas (which will determine future success).

The balanced scorecard splits performance into four "perspectives" for each of which the company should set aims and performance targets.

1 *The financial perspective*
Looking at CM's ability to create wealth, with a particular focus on its shareholders.

Aims would include: increasing profits, reduced risk and survival.

Ratios that could be used would be: return on capital employed, the gearing ratio and current ratio.

2 *The customer perspective*
Looking at CM's ability to satisfy customers (helping to ensure future business).

Aims would include: meeting customers' requirements and high quality.

Ratios that could be used would be: percentage of deliveries on time, percentage of goods returned and percentage of customers placing a repeat order.

3 *The internal business perspective*
Looking at CM's ability to attract and maintain key resources, given the nature of CM's business this would be particularly focused on staff.

Aims would include: successfully recruiting staff, keeping staff and proper maintenance of equipment.

Ratios that could be used would be: percentage vacancies unfilled, staff turnover and percentage time lost due to equipment failures.

4 *The innovation and learning perspective*
Looking at CM's ability to offer new products and solutions to customers and improve its internal procedures.

Aims would include: new products, services and systems.

Ratios that could be used would be: percentage of sales from new products, percentage spending on research that leads to a patent or product and percentage of employee suggestion adopted.

(b) Benchmarking is the use of external actual performance information as a way of evaluating performance and setting targets for management. The information comes from sources external to the business unit (department or division) which may be other business units of the same company or external organisations.

The source of the targets should be "best in class" to ensure that the manager is aspiring to what is both exceptionally good and also feasible.

Benchmarking is normally split into four types.

1 *Internal benchmarking*
This is the use of performance information from one part of an organisation as a target for another part.

CM could use the actual performance of its best performing manufacturing unit as a target for other similar units. Targets could include factors such as defect rates and cost improvements.

2 *External benchmarking*
In this case CM would use external company performance either as an overall target (e.g. HP might be a reasonably similar, exceptional company) or specialised companies or divisions as more specific targets.

Targets, of necessity, would be more general and may include customer satisfaction levels or profitability.

3 *Functional (or activity) benchmarking*
In this case CM would compare particular business functions either internally or externally. This can be across industries.

For example, CM could benchmark its credit control and debtor days between departments and with external companies.

4 *Strategic benchmarking*
CM could observe strategic methods and processes in successful companies, appropriate lessons could be learned and improvements implemented.

CM would be best advised to look at similar companies in rapidly changing business service companies. These need not be in hi-tech business equipment areas, but should share the same customer ethos as CM and experience similar environmental conditions.

May 2007
Questions and
Answers

May 2007 Questions and Answers

14

Managerial Level

Paper P1 – Management Accounting – Performance Evaluation

The answers published here have been written by the Examiner and should provide a helpful guide for both tutors and students.

Published separately on the CIMA website (www.cimaglobal.com/students) from mid-September 2007 is a Post Examination Guide for this paper, which provides much valuable and complementary material including indicative mark information.

CIMA

Management Accounting Pillar

Managerial Level Paper

P1 – Management Accounting – Performance Evaluation

22 May 2007 – Tuesday Morning Session

Instructions to candidates

You are allowed three hours to answer this question paper.
You are allowed 20 minutes reading time **before the examination begins** during which you should read the question paper and, if you wish, highlight and/or make notes on the question paper. However, you will **not** be allowed, **under any circumstances**, to open the answer book and start writing or use your calculator during the reading time.
You are strongly advised to carefully read ALL the question requirements before attempting the question concerned (that is, all parts and/or sub-questions). The requirements for the questions in Section C are contained in a dotted box.
ALL answers must be written in the answer book. Answers or notes written on the question paper will **not** be submitted for marking.
Answer the ONE compulsory question in Section A. This has 15 sub-questions and is on pages 191 to 197.
Answer ALL SIX compulsory sub-questions in Section B on pages 198 and 199.
Answer ONE of the two questions in Section C on pages 200 to 203.
Maths Tables and Formulae are provided on pages 204 to 208.
The list of verbs as published in the syllabus is given for reference on the inside back cover of this question paper.
Write your candidate number, the paper number and examination subject title in the spaces provided on the front of the answer book. Also write your contact ID and name in the space provided in the right hand margin and seal to close.
Tick the appropriate boxes on the front of the answer book to indicate which questions you have answered.

SECTION A – 40 MARKS

[the indicative time for answering this section is 72 minutes]

ANSWER *ALL* FIFTEEN SUB-QUESTIONS

Instructions for answering Section A:

The answers to the fifteen sub-questions in Section A should ALL be written in your answer book.

Your answers should be clearly numbered with the sub-question number then ruled off, so that the markers know which sub-question you are answering. **For multiple choice questions, you need only write the sub-question number and the letter of the answer option you have chosen.** You do not need to start a new page for each sub-question.

For sub-questions **1.11 to 1.15** you should show your workings as marks are available for the method you use to answer these sub-questions.

Question One

1.1   Which of the following best describes an investment centre?

A   A centre for which managers are accountable only for costs.

B   A centre for which managers are accountable only for financial outputs in the form of generating sales revenue.

C   A centre for which managers are accountable for profit.

D   A centre for which managers are accountable for profit and current and non-current assets.

(2 marks)

1.2   A flexible budget is

A   a budget which, by recognising different cost behaviour patterns, is designed to change as volume of activity changes.

B   a budget for a twelve month period which includes planned revenues, expenses, assets and liabilities.

C   a budget which is prepared for a rolling period which is reviewed monthly, and updated accordingly.

D   a budget for semi-variable overhead costs only.

(2 marks)

1.3   The term "budget slack" refers to the

A   lead time between the preparation of the master budget and the commencement of the budget period.

B   difference between the budgeted output and the actual output achieved.

C   additional capacity available which is budgeted for even though it may not be used.

D   deliberate overestimation of costs and/or underestimation of revenues in a budget.

(2 marks)

1.4   PP Ltd is preparing the production and material purchases budgets for one of their products, the SUPERX, for the forthcoming year.

The following information is available:

SUPERX
Sales demand (units)	30,000
Material usage per unit	7 kgs
Estimated opening inventory	3,500 units
Required closing inventory	35% higher than opening inventory

How many units of the SUPERX will need to be produced?

A   28,775

B   30,000

C   31,225

D   38,225

(2 marks)

The following data are given for sub-questions 1.5 and 1.6 below

X Ltd operates a standard costing system and absorbs fixed overheads on the basis of machine hours. Details of budgeted and actual figures are as follows:

	Budget	*Actual*
Fixed overheads	£2,500,000	£2,010,000
Output	500,000 units	440,000 units
Machine hours	1,000,000 hours	900,000 hours

1.5 The fixed overhead expenditure variance is

A   £190,000 favourable

B   £250,000 adverse

C   £300,000 adverse

D   £490,000 favourable

(2 marks)

1.6 The fixed overhead volume variance is

A   £190,000 favourable

B   £250,000 adverse

C   £300,000 adverse

D   £490,000 favourable

(2 marks)

1.7 A company operates a standard absorption costing system. The budgeted fixed production overheads for the company for the latest year were £330,000 and budgeted output was 220,000 units. At the end of the company's financial year the total of the fixed production overheads debited to the Fixed Production Overhead Control Account was £260,000 and the actual output achieved was 200,000 units.

The under / over absorption of overheads was

A   £40,000 over absorbed

B   £40,000 under absorbed

C   £70,000 over absorbed

D   £70,000 under absorbed

(2 marks)

1.8 A company operates a standard absorption costing system. The following fixed production overhead data are available for the latest period:

Budgeted Output	300,000 units
Budgeted Fixed Production Overhead	£1,500,000
Actual Fixed Production Overhead	£1,950,000
Fixed Production Overhead Total Variance	£150,000 adverse

The actual level of production for the period was nearest to

A   277,000 units

B   324,000 units

C   360,000 units

D   420,000 units

(2 marks)

1.9 Which of the following best describes a basic standard?

A   A standard set at an ideal level, which makes no allowance for normal losses, waste and machine downtime.

B   A standard which assumes an efficient level of operation, but which includes allowances for factors such as normal loss, waste and machine downtime.

C   A standard which is kept unchanged over a period of time.

D   A standard which is based on current price levels.

(2 marks)

1.10 XYZ Ltd is preparing the production budget for the next period. The total costs of production are a semi-variable cost. The following cost information has been collected in connection with production:

Volume (units)	Cost
4,500	£29,000
6,500	£33,000

The estimated total production costs for a production volume of 5,750 units is nearest to

A   £29,200

B   £30,000

C   £31,500

D   £32,500

(2 marks)

1.11 S Ltd manufactures three products, A, B and C. The products use a series of different machines but there is a common machine, P, that is a bottleneck.

The selling price and standard cost for each product for the forthcoming year is as follows:

	A $	B $	C $
Selling price	200	150	150
Direct materials	41	20	30
Conversion costs	55	40	66
Machine P – minutes	12	10	7

Calculate the return per hour for each of the products.

(4 marks)

1.12 The following data have been extracted from a company's year-end accounts:

	£
Turnover	7,055,016
Gross profit	4,938,511
Operating profit	3,629,156
Non-current assets	4,582,000
Cash at bank	4,619,582
Short term borrowings	949,339
Trade receivables	442,443
Trade payables	464,692

Calculate the following four performance measures:

(i)   Operating profit margin;
(ii)   Return on capital employed;
(iii)   Trade receivable days (debtors days);
(iv)   Current (Liquidity) ratio.

(4 marks)

1.13 PQR Ltd operates a standard absorption costing system. Details of budgeted and actual figures are as follows:

	Budget	Actual
Sales volume (units)	100,000	110,000
Selling price per unit	£10	£9.50
Variable cost per unit	£5	£5.25
Total cost per unit	£8	£8.30

(i) Calculate the sales price variance.

(2 marks)

(ii) Calculate the sales volume profit variance.

(2 marks)

1.14 WX has two divisions, Y and Z. The following budgeted information is available.

Division Y manufactures motors and budgets to transfer 60,000 motors to Division Z and to sell 40,000 motors to external customers.

Division Z assembles food mixers and uses one motor for each food mixer produced.

The standard cost information per motor for Division Y is as follows:

	£
Direct materials	70
Direct labour	20
Variable production overhead	10
Fixed production overhead	40
Fixed selling and administration overhead	10
Total standard cost	150

In order to set the external selling price the company uses a 33·33% mark up on total standard cost.

(i) Calculate the budgeted profit/(loss) for Division Y if the transfer price is set at marginal cost.

(ii) Calculate the budgeted profit/(loss) for Division Y if the transfer price is set at the total production cost.

(4 marks)

1.15 RF Ltd is about to launch a new product in June 2007. The company has commissioned some market research to assist in sales forecasting. The resulting research and analysis established the following equation:

$Y = Ax^{0.6}$

Where Y is the cumulative sales units, A is the sales units in month 1, $\times$ is the month number.
June 2007 is Month 1.
Sales in June 2007 will be 1,500 units.

Calculate the forecast sales volume for each of the months June, July and August 2007 and for that three month period in total.

(4 marks)

(Total for Section A = 40 marks)

SECTION B – 30 MARKS

[the indicative time for answering this section is 54 minutes]

ANSWER *ALL* SIX SUB-QUESTIONS. EACH SUB-QUESTION IS WORTH 5 MARKS

[?] Question Two

(a) A company uses variance analysis to monitor the performance of the team of workers which assembles Product M. Details of the budgeted and actual performance of the team for last period were as follows:

	Budget	Actual
Output of product M	600 units	680 units
Wage rate	£30 per hour	£32 per hour
Labour hours	900 hours	1,070 hours

It has now been established that the standard wage rate should have been £31·20 per hour.

(i) Calculate the labour rate planning variance and calculate the operational labour efficiency variance.

(ii) Explain the major benefit of analysing variances into planning and operational components.

(5 Marks)

(b) Briefly explain three limitations of standard costing in the modern business environment.

(5 Marks)

(c) Briefly explain three factors that should be considered before deciding to investigate a variance.

(5 Marks)

(d) G Group consists of several autonomous divisions. Two of the divisions supply components and services to other divisions within the group as well as to external clients. The management of G Group is considering the introduction of a bonus scheme for managers that will be based on the profit generated by each division.

Briefly explain the factors that should be considered by the management of G Group when designing the bonus scheme for divisional managers.

(5 Marks)

(e)   Briefly explain the role of a Manufacturing Resource Planning System in supporting a standard costing system.

(5 Marks)

(f)   Briefly explain the main differences between the traditional manufacturing environment and a just-in-time manufacturing environment.

(5 marks)

(Total for Question Two = 30 marks)

(Total for Section B = 30 marks)

SECTION C – 30 MARKS

[the indicative time for answering this section is 54 minutes]

ANSWER *ONE* OF THE TWO QUESTIONS

? Question Three

RJ produces and sells two high performance motor cars: Car X and Car Y. The company operates a standard absorption costing system. The company's budgeted operating statement for the year ending 30 June 2008 and supporting information is given below:

Operating statement year ending 30 June 2008

	Car X $'000	Car Y $'000	Total $'000
Sales	52,500	105,000	157,500
Production cost of sales	40,000	82,250	122,250
Gross profit	12,500	22,750	35,250
Administration costs			
Variable	6,300	12,600	18,900
Fixed	7,000	9,000	16,000
Profit/(loss)	(800)	1,150	350

The production cost of sales for each car was calculated using the following values:

	Car X Units	Car X $'000	Car Y Units	Car Y $'000
Opening inventory	200	8,000	250	11,750
Production	1,100	44,000	1,600	75,200
Closing inventory	300	12,000	100	4,700
Cost of sales	1,000	40,000	1,750	82,250

Production costs
The production costs are made up of direct materials, direct labour, and fixed production overhead. The fixed production overhead is general production overhead (it is not product specific). The total budgeted fixed production overhead is $35,000,000 and is absorbed using a machine hour rate. It takes 200 machine hours to produce one Car X and 300 machine hours to produce one Car Y.

Administration costs
The fixed administration costs include the costs of specific marketing campaigns: $2,000,000 for Car X and $4,000,000 for Car Y.

Requirements

(a) Produce the budgeted operating statement in a marginal costing format.

(7 marks)

(b) Reconcile the total budgeted absorption costing profit with the total budgeted marginal costing profit as shown in the statement you produced in part (a).

(5 marks)

The company is considering changing to an activity based costing system. The company has analysed the budgeted fixed production overheads and found that the costs for various activities are as follows:

	$'000
Machining costs	7,000
Set up costs	12,000
Quality inspections	7,020
Stores receiving	3,480
Stores issues	5,500
	35,000

The analysis also revealed the following information:

	Car X	Car Y
Budgeted production (number of cars)	1,100	1,600
Cars per production run	10	40
Inspections per production run	20	80
Number of component deliveries during the year	492	900
Number of issues from stores	4,000	7,000

Requirements

(c)   Calculate the budgeted production cost of one Car X and one Car Y using the activity based costing information provided above.

(10 marks)

(d)   Prepare a report to the Production Director of RJ which explains the potential benefits of using activity based budgeting for performance evaluation.

(8 marks)

(Total for Question Three = 30 marks)

? Question Four

RF Ltd is a new company which plans to manufacture a specialist electrical component. The company founders will invest £16,250 on the first day of operations, that is, Month 1. They will also transfer fixed capital assets to the company.

The following information is available:

Sales
The forecast sales for the first four months are as follows:

Month	Number of components
1	1,500
2	1,750
3	2,000
4	2,100

The selling price has been set at £10 per component in the first four months.

Sales receipts

Time of payment	% of customers
Month of sale	20*
One month later	45
Two months later	25
Three months later	5

The balance represents anticipated bad debts.

*A 2% discount is given to customers for payment received in the month of sale.

Production
There will be no opening inventory of finished goods in Month 1 but after that it will be policy for the closing inventory to be equal to 20% of the following month's forecast sales.

Variable production cost
The variable production cost is expected to be £6.40 per component.

	£
Direct materials	1.90
Direct wages	3.30
Variable production overheads	1.20
Total variable cost	6.40

Notes:
Direct materials: 100% of the materials required for production will be purchased in the month of production. No inventory of materials will be held. Direct materials will be paid for in the month following purchase.

Direct wages will be paid in the month in which production occurs.

Variable production overheads: 60% will be paid in the month in which production occurs and the remainder will be paid one month later.

Fixed overhead costs
Fixed overhead costs are estimated at £75,000 per annum and are expected to be incurred in equal amounts each month. 60% of the fixed overhead costs will be paid in the month in which they are incurred and 30% in the following month. The balance represents depreciation of fixed assets.

Calculations are to be made to the nearest £1.

Ignore VAT and Tax.

Requirements

(a)   Prepare a cash budget for each of the first three months and in total.

(15 marks)

(b)   There is some uncertainty about the direct material cost. It is thought that the direct material cost per component could range between £1.50 and £2.20. Calculate the budgeted total net cash flow for the three month period if the cost of the direct material is:

(i)   £1.50 per component; or
(ii)   £2.20 per component.

(6 marks)

(c)   Using your answers to part (a) and (b) above, prepare a report to the management of RF Ltd that discusses the benefits or otherwise of performing 'what if' analysis when preparing cash budgets.

(9 marks)

(Total for Question Four = 30 marks)

(Total for Section C = 30 marks)

AREA UNDER THE NORMAL CURVE

This table gives the area under the normal curve between the mean and a point Z standard deviations above the mean. The corresponding area for deviations below the mean can be found by symmetry.

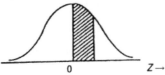

$Z = \dfrac{(x - \mu)}{\sigma}$	0.00	0.01	0.02	0.03	0.04	0.05	0.06	0.07	0.08	0.09
0.0	.0000	.0040	.0080	.0120	.0159	.0199	.0239	.0279	.0319	.0359
0.1	.0398	.0438	.0478	.0517	.0557	.0596	.0636	.0675	.0714	.0753
0.2	.0793	.0832	.0871	.0910	.0948	.0987	.1026	.1064	.1103	.1141
0.3	.1179	.1217	.1255	.1293	.1331	.1368	.1406	.1443	.1480	.1517
0.4	.1554	.1591	.1628	.1664	.1700	.1736	.1772	.1808	.1844	.1879
0.5	.1915	.1950	.1985	.2019	.2054	.2088	.2123	.2157	.2190	.2224
0.6	.2257	.2291	.2324	.2357	.2389	.2422	.2454	.2486	.2518	.2549
0.7	.2580	.2611	.2642	.2673	.2704	.2734	.2764	.2794	.2823	.2852
0.8	.2881	.2910	.2939	.2967	.2995	.3023	.3051	.3078	.3106	.3133
0.9	.3159	.3186	.3212	.3238	.3264	.3289	.3315	.3340	.3365	.3389
1.0	.3413	.3438	.3461	.3485	.3508	.3531	.3554	.3577	.3599	.3621
1.1	.3643	.3665	.3686	.3708	.3729	.3749	.3770	.3790	.3810	.3830
1.2	.3849	.3869	.3888	.3907	.3925	.3944	.3962	.3980	.3997	.4015
1.3	.4032	.4049	.4066	.4082	.4099	.4115	.4131	.4147	.4162	.4177
1.4	.4192	.4207	.4222	.4236	.4251	.4265	.4279	.4292	.4306	.4319
1.5	.4332	.4345	.4357	.4370	.4382	.4394	.4406	.4418	.4430	.4441
1.6	.4452	.4463	.4474	.4485	.4495	.4505	.4515	.4525	.4535	.4545
1.7	.4554	.4564	.4573	.4582	.4591	.4599	.4608	.4616	.4625	.4633
1.8	.4641	.4649	.4656	.4664	.4671	.4678	.4686	.4693	.4699	.4706
1.9	.4713	.4719	.4726	.4732	.4738	.4744	.4750	.4756	.4762	.4767
2.0	.4772	.4778	.4783	.4788	.4793	.4798	.4803	.4808	.4812	.4817
2.1	.4821	.4826	.4830	.4834	.4838	.4842	.4846	.4850	.4854	.4857
2.2	.4861	.4865	.4868	.4871	.4875	.4878	.4881	.4884	.4887	.4890
2.3	.4893	.4896	.4898	.4901	.4904	.4906	.4909	.4911	.4913	.4916
2.4	.4918	.4920	.4922	.4925	.4927	.4929	.4931	.4932	.4934	.4936
2.5	.4938	.4940	.4941	.4943	.4945	.4946	.4948	.4949	.4951	.4952
2.6	.4953	.4955	.4956	.4957	.4959	.4960	.4961	.4962	.4963	.4964
2.7	.4965	.4966	.4967	.4968	.4969	.4970	.4971	.4972	.4973	.4974
2.8	.4974	.4975	.4976	.4977	.4977	.4978	.4979	.4980	.4980	.4981
2.9	.4981	.4982	.4983	.4983	.4984	.4984	.4985	.4985	.4986	.4986
3.0	.49865	.4987	.4987	.4988	.4988	.4989	.4989	.4989	.4990	.4990
3.1	.49903	.4991	.4991	.4991	.4992	.4992	.4992	.4992	.4993	.4993
3.2	.49931	.4993	.4994	.4994	.4994	.4994	.4994	.4995	.4995	.4995
3.3	.49952	.4995	.4995	.4996	.4996	.4996	.4996	.4996	.4996	.4997
3.4	.49966	.4997	.4997	.4997	.4997	.4997	.4997	.4997	.4997	.4998
3.5	.49977									

PRESENT VALUE TABLE

Present value of $1, that is $(1+r)^{-n}$ where r = interest rate; n = number of periods until payment or receipt.

Periods (n)	Interest rates (r)									
	1%	2%	3%	4%	5%	6%	7%	8%	9%	10%
1	0.990	0.980	0.971	0.962	0.952	0.943	0.935	0.926	0.917	0.909
2	0.980	0.961	0.943	0.925	0.907	0.890	0.873	0.857	0.842	0.826
3	0.971	0.942	0.915	0.889	0.864	0.840	0.816	0.794	0.772	0.751
4	0.961	0.924	0.888	0.855	0.823	0.792	0.763	0.735	0.708	0.683
5	0.951	0.906	0.863	0.822	0.784	0.747	0.713	0.681	0.650	0.621
6	0.942	0.888	0.837	0.790	0.746	0705	0.666	0.630	0.596	0.564
7	0.933	0.871	0.813	0.760	0.711	0.665	0.623	0.583	0.547	0.513
8	0.923	0.853	0.789	0.731	0.677	0.627	0.582	0.540	0.502	0.467
9	0.914	0.837	0.766	0.703	0.645	0.592	0.544	0.500	0.460	0.424
10	0.905	0.820	0.744	0.676	0.614	0.558	0.508	0.463	0.422	0.386
11	0.896	0.804	0.722	0.650	0.585	0.527	0.475	0.429	0.388	0.350
12	0.887	0.788	0.701	0.625	0.557	0.497	0.444	0.397	0.356	0.319
13	0.879	0.773	0.681	0.601	0.530	0.469	0.415	0.368	0.326	0.290
14	0.870	0.758	0.661	0.577	0.505	0.442	0.388	0.340	0.299	0.263
15	0.861	0.743	0.642	0.555	0.481	0.417	0.362	0.315	0.275	0.239
16	0.853	0.728	0.623	0.534	0.458	0.394	0.339	0.292	0.252	0.218
17	0.844	0.714	0.605	0.513	0.436	0.371	0.317	0.270	0.231	0.198
18	0.836	0.700	0.587	0.494	0.416	0.350	0.296	0.250	0.212	0.180
19	0.828	0.686	0.570	0.475	0.396	0.331	0.277	0.232	0.194	0.164
20	0.820	0.673	0.554	0.456	0.377	0.312	0.258	0.215	0.178	0.149

Periods (n)	Interest rates (r)									
	11%	12%	13%	14%	15%	16%	17%	18%	19%	20%
1	0.901	0.893	0.885	0.877	0.870	0.862	0.855	0.847	0.840	0.833
2	0.812	0.797	0.783	0.769	0.756	0.743	0.731	0.718	0.706	0.694
3	0.731	0.712	0.693	0.675	0.658	0.641	0.624	0.609	0.593	0.579
4	0.659	0.636	0.613	0.592	0.572	0.552	0.534	0.516	0.499	0.482
5	0.593	0.567	0.543	0.519	0.497	0.476	0.456	0.437	0.419	0.402
6	0.535	0.507	0.480	0.456	0.432	0.410	0.390	0.370	0.352	0.335
7	0.482	0.452	0.425	0.400	0.376	0.354	0.333	0.314	0.296	0.279
8	0.434	0.404	0.376	0.351	0.327	0.305	0.285	0.266	0.249	0.233
9	0.391	0.361	0.333	0.308	0.284	0.263	0.243	0.225	0.209	0.194
10	0.352	0.322	0.295	0.270	0.247	0.227	0.208	0.191	0.176	0.162
11	0.317	0.287	0.261	0.237	0.215	0.195	0.178	0.162	0.148	0.135
12	0.286	0.257	0.231	0.208	0.187	0.168	0.152	0.137	0.124	0.112
13	0.258	0.229	0.204	0.182	0.163	0.145	0.130	0.116	0.104	0.093
14	0.232	0.205	0.181	0.160	0.141	0.125	0.111	0.099	0.088	0.078
15	0.209	0.183	0.160	0.140	0.123	0.108	0.095	0.084	0.079	0.065
16	0.188	0.163	0.141	0.123	0.107	0.093	0.081	0.071	0.062	0.054
17	0.170	0.146	0.125	0.108	0.093	0.080	0.069	0.060	0.052	0.045
18	0.153	0.130	0.111	0.095	0.081	0.069	0.059	0.051	0.044	0.038
19	0.138	0.116	0.098	0.083	0.070	0.060	0.051	0.043	0.037	0.031
20	0.124	0.104	0.087	0.073	0.061	0.051	0.043	0.037	0.031	0.026

Cumulative present value of $1 per annum, Receivable or Payable at the end of each year for n years $\frac{1-(1+r)^{-n}}{r}$

Periods	Interest rates (r)									
(n)	1%	2%	3%	4%	5%	6%	7%	8%	9%	10%
1	0.990	0.980	0.971	0.962	0.952	0.943	0.935	0.926	0.917	0.909
2	1.970	1.942	1.913	1.886	1.859	1.833	1.808	1.783	1.759	1.736
3	2.941	2.884	2.829	2.775	2.723	2.673	2.624	2.577	2.531	2.487
4	3.902	3.808	3.717	3.630	3.546	3.465	3.387	3.312	3.240	3.170
5	4.853	4.713	4.580	4.452	4.329	4.212	4.100	3.993	3.890	3.791
6	5.795	5.601	5.417	5.242	5.076	4.917	4.767	4.623	4.486	4.355
7	6.728	6.472	6.230	6.002	5.786	5.582	5.389	5.206	5.033	4.868
8	7.652	7.325	7.020	6.733	6.463	6.210	5.971	5.747	5.535	5.335
9	8.566	8.162	7.786	7.435	7.108	6.802	6.515	6.247	5.995	5.759
10	9.471	8.983	8.530	8.111	7.722	7.360	7.024	6.710	6.418	6.145
11	10.368	9.787	9.253	8.760	8.306	7.887	7.499	7.139	6.805	6.495
12	11.255	10.575	9.954	9.385	8.863	8.384	7.943	7.536	7.161	6.814
13	12.134	11.348	10.635	9.986	9.394	8.853	8.358	7.904	7.487	7.103
14	13.004	12.106	11.296	10.563	9.899	9.295	8.745	8.244	7.786	7.367
15	13.865	12.849	11.938	11.118	10.380	9.712	9.108	8.559	8.061	7.606
16	14.718	13.578	12.561	11.652	10.838	10.106	9.447	8.851	8.313	7.824
17	15.562	14.292	13.166	12.166	11.274	10.477	9.763	9.122	8.544	8.022
18	16.398	14.992	13.754	12.659	11.690	10.828	10.059	9.372	8.756	8.201
19	17.226	15.679	14.324	13.134	12.085	11.158	10.336	9.604	8.950	8.365
20	18.046	16.351	14.878	13.590	12.462	11.470	10.594	9.818	9.129	8.514

Periods	Interest rates (r)									
(n)	11%	12%	13%	14%	15%	16%	17%	18%	19%	20%
1	0.901	0.893	0.885	0.877	0.870	0.862	0.855	0.847	0.840	0.833
2	1.713	1.690	1.668	1.647	1.626	1.605	1.585	1.566	1.547	1.528
3	2.444	2.402	2.361	2.322	2.283	2.246	2.210	2.174	2.140	2.106
4	3.102	3.037	2.974	2.914	2.855	2.798	2.743	2.690	2.639	2.589
5	3.696	3.605	3.517	3.433	3.352	3.274	3.199	3.127	3.058	2.991
6	4.231	4.111	3.998	3.889	3.784	3.685	3.589	3.498	3.410	3.326
7	4.712	4.564	4.423	4.288	4.160	4.039	3.922	3.812	3.706	3.605
8	5.146	4.968	4.799	4.639	4.487	4.344	4.207	4.078	3.954	3.837
9	5.537	5.328	5.132	4.946	4.772	4.607	4.451	4.303	4.163	4.031
10	5.889	5.650	5.426	5.216	5.019	4.833	4.659	4.494	4.339	4.192
11	6.207	5.938	5.687	5.453	5.234	5.029	4.836	4.656	4.486	4.327
12	6.492	6.194	5.918	5.660	5.421	5.197	4.988	7.793	4.611	4.439
13	6.750	6.424	6.122	5.842	5.583	5.342	5.118	4.910	4.715	4.533
14	6.982	6.628	6.302	6.002	5.724	5.468	5.229	5.008	4.802	4.611
15	7.191	6.811	6.462	6.142	5.847	5.575	5.324	5.092	4.876	4.675
16	7.379	6.974	6.604	6.265	5.954	5.668	5.405	5.162	4.938	4.730
17	7.549	7.120	6.729	6.373	6.047	5.749	5.475	5.222	4.990	4.775
18	7.702	7.250	6.840	6.467	6.128	5.818	5.534	5.273	5.033	4.812
19	7.839	7.366	6.938	6.550	6.198	5.877	5.584	5.316	5.070	4.843
20	7.963	7.469	7.025	6.623	6.259	5.929	5.628	5.353	5.101	4.870

Formulae

PROBABILITY

$A \cup B = $ **A or B**. $A \cap B = $ **A and B** (overlap).

$P(B \mid A) = $ probability of B, **given** A.

Rules of Addition

If A and B are mutually exclusive: $P(A \cup B) = P(A) + P(B)$

If A and B are **not** mutually exclusive: $P(A \cup B) = P(A) + P(B) - P(A \cap B)$

Rules of Multiplication

If A and B are *independent*: $P(A \cap B) = P(A) * P(B)$

If A and B are **not** *independent*: $P(A \cap B) = P(A) * P(B \mid A)$

$E(X) = \sum (\text{probability} * \text{payoff})$

Quadratic Equations

If $aX^2 + bX + c = 0$ is the general quadratic equation, the two solutions (roots) are given by:

$$X = \frac{-b \pm \sqrt{b^2 - 4ac}}{2a}$$

DESCRIPTIVE STATISTICS

Arithmetic Mean

$$\bar{x} = \frac{\sum x}{n} \qquad \bar{x} = \frac{\sum fx}{\sum f} \quad \text{(frequency distribution)}$$

Standard Deviation

$$SD = \sqrt{\frac{\sum (x - \bar{x})^2}{n}} \qquad SD = \sqrt{\frac{\sum fx^2}{\sum f} - \overline{x^2}} \quad \text{(frequency distribution)}$$

INDEX NUMBERS

Price relative = $100 * P_1/P_0$ Quantity relative = $100 * Q_1/Q_0$

Price:
$$\frac{\sum w * \left(\dfrac{P_1}{P_0} \right)}{\sum w} \times 100$$

Quantity:
$$\frac{\sum w * \left(\dfrac{Q_1}{Q_0} \right)}{\sum w} \times 100$$

TIME SERIES

Additive Model

Series = Trend + Seasonal + Random

Multiplicative Model

Series = Trend * Seasonal * Random

LINEAR REGRESSION AND CORRELATION

The linear regression equation of Y on X is given by:

$$Y = a + bX \quad or \quad Y - \overline{Y} = b(X - \overline{X})$$

where

$$b = \frac{\text{Covariance}(XY)}{\text{Variance}(X)} = \frac{n \sum XY - (\sum X)(\sum Y)}{n \sum X^2 - (\sum X)^2}$$

and

$$a = \overline{Y} - b\overline{X}$$

or solve

$$\sum Y = na + b \sum X$$
$$\sum XY = a \sum X + b\sum X^2$$

Coefficient of correlation

$$r = \frac{\text{Covariance}(XY)}{\sqrt{\text{Var}(X).\text{Var}(Y)}} = \frac{n \sum XY - (\sum X)(\sum Y)}{\sqrt{\{n \sum X^2 - (\sum X)^2\}\{n \sum Y^2 - (\sum Y)^2\}}}$$

$$R(\text{rank}) = 1 - \frac{6 \sum d^2}{n(n^2 - 1)}$$

FINANCIAL MATHEMATICS

Compound Interest (Values and Sums)

Future Value S, of a sum of X, invested for n periods, compounded at $r\%$ interest

$$S = X[1 + r]^n$$

Annuity

Present value of an annuity of £1 per annum receivable or payable for n years, commencing in one year, discounted at $r\%$ per annum:

$$PV = \frac{1}{r}\left[1 - \frac{1}{[1+r]^n}\right]$$

Perpetuity

Present value of £1 per annum, payable or receivable in perpetuity, commencing in one year, discounted at $r\%$ per annum:

$$PV = \frac{1}{r}$$

LIST OF VERBS USED IN THE QUESTION REQUIREMENTS

A list of the learning objectives and verbs that appear in the syllabus and in the question requirements for each question in this paper.

It is important that you answer the question according to the definition of the verb.

LEARNING OBJECTIVE	VERBS USED	DEFINITION
1 KNOWLEDGE		
What you are expected to know.	List	Make a list of
	State	Express, fully or clearly, the details of/facts of
	Define	Give the exact meaning of
2 COMPREHENSION		
What you are expected to understand.	Describe	Communicate the key features
	Distinguish	Highlight the differences between
	Explain	Make clear or intelligible/State the meaning of
	Identify	Recognise, establish or select after consideration
	Illustrate	Use an example to describe or explain something
3 APPLICATION		
How you are expected to apply your knowledge.	Apply	To put to practical use
	Calculate/compute	To ascertain or reckon mathematically
	Demonstrate	To prove with certainty or to exhibit by practical means
	Prepare	To make or get ready for use
	Reconcile	To make or prove consistent/compatible
	Solve	Find an answer to
	Tabulate	Arrange in a table
4 ANALYSIS		
How are you expected to analyse the detail of what you have learned.	Analyse	Examine in detail the structure of
	Categorise	Place into a defined class or division
	Compare and contrast	Show the similarities and/or differences between
	Construct	To build up or compile
	Discuss	To examine in detail by argument
	Interpret	To translate into intelligible or familiar terms
	Produce	To create or bring into existence
5 EVALUATION		
How are you expected to use your learning to evaluate, make decisions or recommendations.	Advise	To counsel, inform or notify
	Evaluate	To appraise or assess the value of
	Recommend	To advise on a course of action

The Examiner for Management Accounting – Performance Evaluation offers to future candidates and to tutors using this booklet for study purposes, the following background and guidance on the questions included in this examination paper.

Section A – Question One – Compulsory

Question One consists of 15 objective test sub-questions. These are drawn from all sections of the syllabus. They are designed to examine breadth across the syllabus and thus cover many learning outcomes.

Section B – Question Two – Compulsory

Question Two has six sub-questions.

(a)   covers learning outcome B(iv) – *Calculate and interpret planning and operational variances.*
(b)   covers learning outcome B (i) – *Explain why and how standards are set in manufacturing and in service industries with particular reference to the maximisation of efficiency and minimisation of waste* and B(ii) – *Calculate and interpret material, labour, variable overhead, fixed overhead and sales variances.*
(c)   covers learning outcome B(ii) – *Calculate and interpret material, labour, variable overhead, fixed overhead and sales variances.*
(d)   covers learning outcome D(v) – *Discuss the likely behavioural consequences of the use of performance metrics in managing cost, profit and investment centres.*
(e)   covers learning outcome A(vii) – *Explain the role of MRP and ERP systems in supporting standard costing systems.*
(f)   covers learning outcome A(viii) – *Evaluate the impact of just-in-time manufacturing methods on cost accounting.*

Section C – answer one of two questions

Question Three has four parts.

(a)   covers learning outcome A(i) – *Compare and contrast marginal and absorption costing methods in respect of profit reporting and stock valuation.*
(b)   covers learning outcome A(i) – *Compare and contrast marginal and absorption costing methods in respect of profit reporting and stock valuation.*
(c)   covers learning outcome A(vi) – *Compare activity-based costing with traditional marginal and absorption costing methods and evaluate its potential as a system of cost accounting.*
(d)   covers learning outcome C(vi) – *Evaluate and apply alternative approaches to budgeting.*

Question Four has three parts.

(a)   covers learning outcome C(iii) – *Calculate projected revenues and costs based on product/service volumes, pricing strategies and cost structures.*
(b)   covers learning outcome C(vii) – *Calculate the consequences of "what if" scenarios and evaluate their impact on master profit and loss account and balance sheet.*
(c)   covers learning outcome C(vii) – *Calculate the consequences of "what if" scenarios and evaluate their impact on master profit and loss account and balance sheet.*

Managerial Level Paper

P1 – Management Accounting – Performance Evaluation

Examiner's Answers

SECTION A

? Question One

1.1 The correct answer is D.

1.2 The correct answer is A.

1.3 The correct answer is D.

1.4

	Units
Sales	30,000
Req'd closing inventory	4,725
Less opening inventory	(3,500)
Production	31,225

The correct answer is C.

1.5

Budget	£2,500,000
Actual	£2,010,000
Variance	£490,000 favourable

The correct answer is D.

1.6

Budgeted volume	500,000 units
Actual volume	440,000 units
	60,000 units

OAR

2 hours × £2.50	× £5 per unit
Volume variance	£300,000 adverse

The correct answer is C.

1.7

	£
Absorbed (200,000 units × £1.50)	300,000
Incurred	260,000
Over absorbed	40,000

The correct answer is A.

1.8 Actual fixed production

overhead cost	£1,950,000
Total variance	£150,000 adverse
Absorbed	£1,800,000
OAR per unit	£5
	360,000 units

The correct answer is C.

1.9 **The correct answer is C.**

1.10					
		High Low Method	*Activity*	*Cost*	
		Highest	6,500	£33,000	
		Lowest	4,500	£29,000	
		Difference	2,000	£4,000	
		Variable cost per unit		£2	
		Substitute into highest activity	6,500	£33,000	Total cost
			6,500 × £2	£13 000	Variable cost
			Difference	£20,000	Fixed cost
		Therefore	5,750 × £2	£11,500	Variable cost
				£20,000	Fixed cost
				£31,500	Total cost

The correct answer is C.

1.11		A	B	C
		$	$	$
	Selling price	200	150	150
	Direct m aterials	41	20	30
	Throughput	159	130	120
	Machine P – minutes per unit	12	10	7
	Return per factory hour			
		159/12	130/10	120/7
		13.25	13	17.14
	× 60 minutes	**795**	**780**	**1 028**

1.12	Operating profit margin	$(3,629,156/7,055,016) \times 100 = 51.44\%$
	Return on capital employed	$[3,629,156/(4,582,000 + 4,619,582 + 442,443 - 949,339 - 464,692)] \times 100 = 44.10\%$
	Trade receivable days	$(442,443/7,055,016) \times 365$ days = 22.89 days
	Current/liquidity ratio	$(4,619,582 + 442,443)/(949,339 + 464,692) = 3.58$ times

1.13	**Sales price variance**		
	Budgeted selling price	£10.00	
	Actual selling price	£9.50	
		£0.50	adverse
	Actual sales volume (units)	110,000	
		£55,000	adverse
	Sales volume profit variance		
	Budgeted sales volume (units)	100,000	
	Actual sales volume (units)	110,000	
		10,000	favourable
	Standard profit per unit	£2	
		£20,000	favourable

1.14

(i)	Budgeted loss – marginal cost transfer price		
	Sales		£'000
	Internal	60,000 × £100	6,000
	External	40,000 × (£150 × 1.3333)	8,000
			14,000
	Variable cost	100,000 × £100	10,000
	Contribution		4,000
	Fixed costs		
	Production	100,000 × £40	4,000
	Administration	100,000 × £10	1,000
	Loss		(1,000)

(ii)	Budgeted profit – absorption cost transfer price		
	Sales		£'000
	Internal	60,000 × £140	8,400
	External	40,000 × (£150 × 1.3333)	8,000
			16,400
	Variable cost	100,000 × £100	10,000
	Contribution		6,400
	Fixed costs		
	Production	100,000 × £40	4,000
	Administration	100,000 × £10	1,000
	Profit		1,400

1.15 Forecast sales volume for June, July and August is:

Month	Cumulative sales (units)	Monthly sales (units)
June	1,500	1,500
July	2,274	774
August	2,900	626

SECTION B

(a)

(i)   Difference in standard wage rate = £1.20 per hour

Planning variance	(standard hours for actual output) × difference in wage rate
	680 × (900/600) × £1.20
	1,020 × £1.20
	£1,224 Adverse
Operational efficiency variance	(standard hours for actual output − actual hours) × revised wage rate
	(1,020 − 1,070) × £31.20
	50 × £31.20
	£1,560 Adverse

(ii)   The major benefit of analysing the variances into planning and operational components is that the revised standard should provide a realistic standard against which to measure performance. Any variances should then be a result of operational management efficiencies and inefficiencies and not faulty planning.

(b)

The main limitations of standard costing in the modern business environment are as follows:

- The business environment in the past was more stable whereas the modern business environment is more dynamic and subject to change. As a result if a business environment is continuously changing standard costing is not a suitable method because standards cannot be established for a reasonable period of time.

- The focus of the modern business environment is on improving quality and customer care whereas the environment in the past was focused on minimising cost.

- The life cycle of products in the modern business environment is shorter and therefore standards become quickly out of date.

- The increase in automation in the modern business environment has resulted in less emphasis on labour cost variances.

(c)

The benefit of investigating a variance should never exceed the cost of investigation. However this can be difficult to ascertain and therefore a manager should decide to investigate a variance based on the following:

Size
Criteria will be laid down which state that variances which are of a certain amount or percentage will be investigated. This is an extremely simple method to apply but the cut off values can be subjective.

Controllable / Uncontrollable
There is little point in investigating a variance if it is uncontrollable. The cost in this situation would outweigh the benefits of investigation since there would be no benefit obtained.

Interrelationships
An adverse variance in one part of the business may result in a favourable variance elsewhere. These interdependencies must be considered when deciding on investigation. For example a favourable labour rate variance may result in an adverse efficiency variance where less skilled workers are employed, costing less, as a result the workers take longer to do the job and an adverse efficiency variance arises.

Type of standard
If a company sets an ideal standard this will usually lead to adverse variances. The manager will need to decide at what size of adverse variance an investigation should take place on such variances.

(d)

Firstly G Group must consider the transfer pricing system. The system must provide information that motivates divisional managers to make good economic decisions not just for themselves but for the company as a whole. It should also provide information that is useful for evaluating the managerial and economic performance of the divisions and should ensure that divisional autonomy is not undermined.

If there is unlimited demand for the output of the two divisions in the market then the transfer price should equal the market price less any savings as a result of internal transfer. This then allows the divisions to report a profit on the transfers and will not cause any issue for the calculation of the bonus.

However, if there is a limit on the amount that can be sold on the external market then the divisions would be transferring at marginal cost as there is no opportunity cost. In this case they will simply cover the marginal cost and have no contribution towards fixed costs or profit. This will mean that if the bonus is awarded on profit the divisional manager will not receive a bonus despite the fact that they have made internal supplies.

Therefore the company must ensure that in order for decisions to remain goal congruent the bonus scheme must allow for internal transfers that impact on the divisions' ability to earn bonuses.

Other areas to consider when implementing a bonus scheme include:

- It should be clearly understood by all personnel involved;
- There should be no delay between the awarding of the bonus and the subsequent payment of the bonus;
- It should motivate the personnel;
- It should not cause sub-optimal behaviour;
- Controllable and uncontrollable costs and revenues should be identified separately.

(e)

A manufacturing resource planning system involves the planning of raw materials, components, subassemblies and other input resources, such as machine capacity and labour, so that the system provides a fully integrated planning approach to the management of all the company's manufacturing resources. The quality of the data which sets the parameters within a manufacturing resource planning system drives the company's operations and determines the optimal production and purchasing plan.

In order to ensure that a manufacturing resource planning system operates effectively it is essential to have:

- A master production schedule, which specifies both the timing and quantity demanded of each of the top-level finished good items.
- A bill of materials file for each sub-assembly, component and part, containing details of the number of items on hand, scheduled receipts and items allocated to released orders but not yet drawn from inventories.
- A master parts file containing planned lead times of all items to be purchased and sub-assemblies and components to be produced internally.
- A master labour and machine capacity file which specifies both the timing and quantity demanded to achieve planned production levels.

The data identified above that is used to ensure the manufacturing resource planning system operates effectively can then be used in a standard costing system to set parameters for materials, labour and overhead capacity. These will then be used to measure performance through variance analysis.

(f)

Just-in-time is a system whose objective is to produce or procure products or components as they are required by a customer or for use, rather than for inventory. A just-in-time system is a 'pull system' which responds to demand, in contrast to a 'push system', in which inventories act as buffers between the different elements of the system, such as purchasing, production and sales.

The traditional business environment is a 'push system' in which one process supplies parts to the next process without regard to the ability to continue work on those parts.

This extends onto producing finished goods inventory ready for sale to customers. Work in progress, inventory of raw materials and finished goods inventory are an inherent part of such a traditional system.

On the other hand a just in time system is described as a philosophy, or approach to management, as it encompasses a commitment to continuous improvement and the pursuit of excellence in the design and operation of the production management system. A JIT system operates in such a way that production and resource acquisition should be pulled by customer demand rather than being pushed by a planning process. A JIT based production operation responds quickly to customer demand and resources are acquired and utilised only when needed. A JIT system operates with little or no inventories and in order to be able to operate in this manner, an organisation must achieve excellence in the following areas:

- Production scheduling
- Supplier relations
- Plant maintenance
- Information systems
- Quality controls
- Customer relations

SECTION C

? Question Three

(a) Total production cost:

Car X = $40,000 (standard unit cost from the table showing information for the cost of sales)
Car Y = $47,000

Fixed production overhead = $35,000,000
Budgeted machine hours = $(1,100 \times 200) + (1,600 \times 300) = 700,000$ machine hours
Fixed production overhead absorption rate = $35,000,000/700,000 = $50 per machine hour.

	Car X $ per car	Car Y $ per car
Total production cost	40,000	47,000
Fixed overhead absorbed	10,000	15,000
Variable production cost per car	30,000	32,000

Marginal costing operating statement – year ending 30 June 2008

	Car X $'000	Car Y $'000	Total $'000
Sales	52,500	105,000	157,500
Variable production costs	30,000	56,000	86,000
Variable administration costs	6,300	12,600	18,900
Contribution	16,200	36,400	52,600
Specific fixed costs			
Marketing	2,000	4,000	6,000
Contribution to general fixed costs	14,200	32,400	46,600
General fixed costs			
Production			35,000
Administration			10,000
Profit			**1,600**

(b) The difference in the profit figures will be caused by the fixed production overheads that are absorbed into closing inventories. Changes in inventory levels will determine the amount of fixed production overheads that are 'moved' into the next accounting period and not charged in this period. If inventory levels increase, the absorption costing profit will be higher than the profit calculated using marginal costing.

	Car X	Car Y
Opening inventory (units)	200	250
Closing inventory (units)	300	100
Change in inventory (units)	+100	−150
Marginal profit will be	lower	higher
Fixed production overhead per car	$10,000	$15,000
Total difference in profits	$1,000,000	$2,250,000
Reconciliation		
	$'000	
Absorption costing profit	350	
Car X: inventory impact	(1,000)	
Car Y: inventory impact	2,250	
Marginal costing profit	1,600	

(c)

Activity	Cost Driver	Calculation of drivers	Drivers
Machining costs	Machine hours	700,000	700,000
Set up costs	No. of production runs	(1,100/10) + (1,600/40)	150
Quality inspections	No. of inspections	(110 x 20) + (40 × 80)	5,400
Stores receiving	No. of deliveries	492 + 900	1,392
Stores issues	No. of issues	4,000 + 7,000	11,000

Activity	$'000	Driver	Cost per driver
Machining costs	7,000	700,000	$10 per machine hour
Set up costs	12,000	150	$80,000 per set up
Quality inspections	7,020	5,400	$1,300 per inspection
Stores receiving	3,480	1,392	$2,500 per delivery
Stores issues	5,500	11,000	$500 per issue

	Car X		Car Y	
	Driver	$'000	Driver	$'000
Machining costs	220,000	2,200	480,000	4,800
Set up costs	110	8,800	40	3,200
Quality inspections	2,200	2,860	3,200	4,160
Stores receiving	492	1,230	900	2,250
Stores issues	4,000	2,000	7,000	3,500
Total overhead		17,090		17,910
Direct costs		33,000		51,200
Total production costs		50,090		69,110
Cars produced		1,100		1,600
Cost per car		**$45,536**		**$43,194**

(d)

Report

To: Production Director
From: Management Accountant
Date: 22 May 2007
Subject: Activity Based Budgeting – Performance Evaluation

As you are aware we are considering the implementation of an activity based costing system and moving away from the traditional absorption costing system which we currently operate.

There are many potential benefits associated with implementing activity based budgeting (ABB) for performance evaluation. Please find below an outline of some of the benefits that can be achieved from ABB.

Preparing budgets using a traditional absorption costing approach involves presenting costs under functional headings, that is, costs are presented in a manner that emphasises their nature. The weakness of this approach is that it gives little indication of the link between the level of activity of the department and the cost incurred. In contrast, activity based budgeting provides a clear framework for understanding the link between costs and the level of activity. This would allow us to evaluate performance based on the activity that drives the cost.

The modern business environment has a high proportion of costs that are indirect and the only meaningful way of attributing these costs to individual products is to find the root cause of such costs, that is, what activity is driving these costs. The traditional absorption costing approach does not provide this level of detail as costs under this system are attributed to individual products using a volume related measure. For our company this is machine hours which results in an arbitrary product cost. This makes it difficult to hold individual managers accountable for variances that arise. Whereas with an activity based costing approach responsibility can be broken down and assigned accordingly and individual managers can provide input into the budgeting process and subsequently be held responsible for the variances arising.

There is greater transparency with an ABB system due to the level of detail behind the costs. The traditional absorption costing approach combines all of the overheads together using a machine hour basis to calculate an overhead absorption rate and uses this rate to attribute overheads to products. ABB will drill down in much more detail examining the cost and the driver of such costs and calculates a cost driver rate which will be used to assign overheads to products. Therefore ABB has greater transparency than absorption costing and allows for much more detailed information on overhead consumption and so on. This then lends itself to better performance evaluation.

I would like to conclude that the traditional absorption costing approach to product costing does not enable us to provide a satisfactory explanation for the behaviour of costs. In contrast ABB will provide such details which will allow us to have better cost control, improved performance evaluation and greater manager accountability.

If you require any further information please do not hesitate to contact me.

? Question Four

(a)

Cash Budget

	Month 1 £	Month 2 £	Month 3 £	Total £
Sales receipts	2,940	10,180	15,545	28,665
Capital injection	16,250			16,250
Total receipts	**19,190**	**10,180**	**15,545**	**44,915**
Outflow				
Materials	0	3,515	3,420	6,935
Labour	6,105	5,940	6,666	18,711
Variable overhead	1,332	2,184	2,318	5,834
Fixed overhead	3,750	5,625	5,625	15,000
Total Outflow	**11,187**	**17,264**	**18,029**	**46,480**
Inflow-Outflow	8,003	(7,084)	(2,484)	(1,565)
Bal b/fwd	0	8,003	919	0
Bal c/fwd	8,003	919	(1,565)	(1,565)

Workings

Sales receipts	1	2	3
Sales units	1,500	1,750	2,000
	£	£	£
Selling price	10	10	10
Sales	15,000	17,500	20,000
Paid in month – 20%	3,000	3,500	4,000
Discount paid in month 2%	−60	−70	−80
45% in the following month		6,750	7,875
25% in 3rd month			3,750
Receipts	**2,940**	**10,180**	**15,545**

Production	1 units	2 units	3 units	4 units
Required by sales	1,500	1,750	2,000	2,100
Opening inventory		(350)	(400)	
	1,500	1,400	1,600	
Closing inventory	350	400	420	
Production	1,850	1,800	2,020	
Material price	£1.90	£1.90	£1.90	
Material cost	£3,515	£3,420	£3,838	
Payment		£3,515	£3,420	

Labour			
Production units	1,850	1,800	2,020
Rate per unit	£3.30	£3.30	£3.30
Payment	£6,105	£5,940	£6,666

Variable Overhead

Production units	1,850	1,800	2,020
Rate per unit	£1.20	£1.20	£1.20
Variable overhead cost	£2,220	£2,160	£2,424
Payment	£	£	£
60% in month	1,332	1,296	1,454
40% in following month		888	864
Payment	**1,332**	**2,184**	**2,318**
Fixed overhead	6,250	6,250	6,250
Payment			
60% in month	3,750	3,750	3,750
30% in following month		1,875	1,875
Payment	**3,750**	**5,625**	**5,625**

(b)

(i)

	Month 1	Month 2	Month 3
£1.50			
£1.50 – £1.90	£0.40	£0.40	£0.40
Production units	1,850	1,800	2,020
Saving	£740	£720	£808
Saving		£740	£720
Total cash benefit	£1,460		
Current cash flow at £1.90	£(1,565)		
Revised cash flow at £1.50	**£(105)**		

(ii)

	Month 1	Month 2	Month 3
£2.20			
£2.20 – £1.90	£0.30	£0.30	£0.30
Production units	1,850	1,800	2,020
Additional cost	£555	£540	£606
Payment		£555	£540
Total additional payment	£1,095		
Current cash flow at £1.90	£(1,565)		
Revised cash flow at £2.20	**£(2,660)**		

(c)

Report

To: Management

From: Management Accountant

Date: 22 May 2007

Subject: 'What if' analysis and cash budgets

This report addresses the benefits or otherwise of 'what if' analysis in relation to cash budgets. When there is a degree of uncertainty concerning elements incorporated within a budget 'what if' analysis allows us to revise the budgets on the basis of a series of varied assumptions.

In preparing the cash budgets we have identified that there is a degree of uncertainty concerning the direct material cost.   We have used assumptions in part (b) to perform some calculations to estimate the effect of this uncertainty on the budgeted cash flow.   The results were as follows:

Direct material cost per component	Increase/(decrease) in cash flow	Budgeted cash flow
£2.20	(£1,095)	(£2,660)
£1.50	£1,460	(£105)
£1.90		(£1,565)

If we perform some 'what if' analysis around these figures we can determine that a direct material cost of £2.20, that is, a 16% increase in material cost, results in a negative cash flow of −£2,660.   This is a 70% increase in the closing cash negative balance.   A direct material cost of £1.50, that is, a 21% decrease in direct material cost, results in a revised cashflow of −£105.   This is a 93% reduction in the closing cash negative balance.

The benefits of 'what if' analysis are that it allows us to:

- assess how responsive the cash flow is to changes in variables.   Therefore we can assess how sensitive the variable is to changing conditions.   From our calculations above obviously if the material cost increases it has a significant impact on the closing cash position;
- review critical variables to assess whether or not there is a strong possibility of the event occurring which leads to a negative cash flow;
- assess the variables that are most sensitive.   These are the variables which cause the greatest variation with the lowest percentage change.   It is important for the founders to pay particular attention to such variables and carefully monitor them.

It should however be noted that there are serious limitations when using 'what if' analysis'.   Two of the major ones are as follows.

- The changes in key variables are isolated whereas the management will be more interested in the effect on the cash flow of two or more key variables changing;
- There is no indication of the likelihood of a key variable changing and therefore the use of 'what if' analysis is limited.

Should you require any further analysis or information please do not hesitate to contact me.